Surface Decoration
for Low-Fire Ceramics

Surface Decoration

for Low-Fire Ceramics

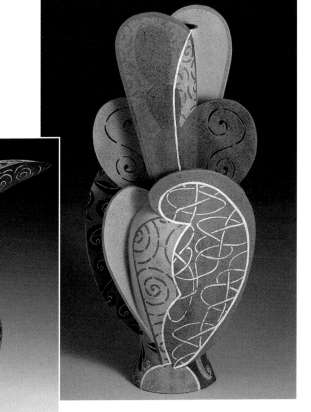

Slips

Terra Sigillata

Underglazes

Glazes

Maiolica

Overglaze Enamels

Decals

Lynn Peters

LARK BOOKS

A Division of Sterling Publishing Co., Inc.
New York

This book is dedicated to
Larry and Germaine Peters.

Editor: **Katherine M. Duncan**
Art Direction: **Kathleen Holmes**
Editorial Assistants: **Heather Smith, Catharine Sutherland**
Editorial Intern: **Jennifer Jenkins**
Production: **Kathleen Holmes**
Production Assistant: **Hannes Charen**
Photography (techniques): **Evan Bracken**
Additional Photography: **Glen Carpenter**

Library of Congress Cataloging-in-Publication Data
Peters, Lynn.
    Surface decoration for low-fire ceramics : slips, terra sigillata, underglazes,
glazes, maiolica, decals / Lynn Peters.
      p. cm.
    Includes bibliographical references and index.
    ISBN 1-57990-270-7
    1. Glazes.   2. Glazing (Ceramics)   I. Title.
TP812.P47   1999
738.1'27—dc21
                              98-30906
                                  CIP

10 9 8 7 6 5 4 3 2 1

Published by Lark Books, a division of
Sterling Publishing Co., Inc.
387 Park Avenue South, New York, N.Y. 10016

© 1999 by Lynn Peters

Distributed in Canada by Sterling Publishing,
c/o Canadian Manda Group, One Atlantic Ave., Suite 105
Toronto, Ontario, Canada M6K 3E7

Distributed in Australia by Capricorn Link (Australia) Pty Ltd., P.O.
Box 6651, Baulkham Hills, Business Centre
NSW 2153, Australia

Distributed in the U.K. by:
Guild of Master Craftsman Publications Ltd.
Castle Place 166 High Street, Lewes, East Sussex, England, BN7 1XU
Tel: (+ 44) 1273 477374 Fax: (+ 44) 1273 478606
Email: pubs@thegmcgroup.com, Web: www.gmcpublications.com

Pictured on title page (left to right):
Lynn Peters, **Buried Treasure**, 1994.
Andrea Gill, **Persian Ornament**, 1996.
Carol Gouthro, **Tulip Vase**, 1998.

Pictured on contents page:
Lynn Peters, **Amphora**, 1997.

**Pictured on pages 6 and 7
(left to right):**
Michel Louise Conroy, **Teapot**, 1995.
Beverly Crist, **Jack of Diamonds**, 1997.
Mitch Yung, **Twist Buffet Platter**, 1998.
Terry Siebert, **Meadow Pitcher**, 1995.

Images pictured on pages 8, 10, 32,
94, 95, 98, 102, 106, 112, and 116
by Lynn Peters

CONTENTS

INTRODUCTION

Today, the art of surface decoration for ceramics commands the full attention of many potters. Through this book you will discover the world of surface decoration for low-fire ceramics—full of color, texture, and infinite possibilities. The rich "canvas" which clay provides lends itself to techniques such as painting, drawing, stencilling, and carving. A multitude of coverings for clay—made commercially or in the studio—can create designs that are brilliantly colored and intricate.

You'll benefit from the contents of this book whether you're a novice or an experienced ceramicist. A section on clay helps you get started. Another segment of the book explains applications from underglazes to

overglazes, and techniques, such as slip trailing and sgraffito, followed by beautifully illustrated explanations by the author. Throughout the book, a gallery of works created by top ceramicists from the United States, Canada, and Britain will amaze and inspire you.

Working with surface decorations will excite you as you discover new techniques and combinations that are not entirely predictable until fired and taken from the kiln. This element of surprise is a great part of the appeal of painting on a colored slip, layering it with stencils and more slip, and then peeling away the stencils to reveal patterns underneath—all before the final step of firing.

But after it is all said, done, and learned, working with surface decorations is like any other creative endeavor—much of it is an intuitive process, despite technical and rational explanations. After mastering the basics, you'll have a vocabulary from which to launch into the realm of the experimental and improvisational. You may discover a method of doing something that no one else has, all of the techniques that you'll read about on the following pages were at one point uncovered by an inquisitive person who wanted to try something new.

So, sit back and enjoy, but prepare yourself...surface decoration can be addictive!

Pottery is at once the simplest and the most difficult of all the arts.

-Herbert Read

I LOVE POTS WHETHER decorated or not. I love the vessel, the clay, the whole of it. But it is the act of decorating the surface of the pot that places the experience in another realm. Painted pottery tells a story. I'm fascinated with the ability of pattern and imagery to reveal a particular human experience. I feel a connection with the ancient images on the cave walls of Lascaux, the timeless designs of early Greek pottery, and the elegant lines of Minoan amphorae. An irresistible urge to pursue this process, and thus join a long line of storytellers, has sent me on my inquiries.

It was this love of making painterly pottery that inspired me to write this book of clay applications and techniques, so that others can try their hand at surface decoration. The book presents a collection of possibilities for surface decoration on clay fired within the low-fire temperature range.

When I first started making pottery at Sheridan School of Design in Toronto, in the 1970s, the focus of my study was high-fire

reduction ware. Bernard Leach's *A Potter's Book* was the bible that I read while I sat up all night waiting for cone ten to go down. There was a sense of trying to preserve the mysterious art of reduction fire and the tradition of the unknown craftsman.

The fabrication of the piece was the place of impact for the artist. Glazes such as spodumene, tenmoku, and celadon predominated. Salt fire surfaces, wood fire deposits of ashes, or flashing were the *shibui wabe*, or happy accidents, to which we aspired. Glazing and other surface treatments were a detached process and a function of practicality.

During this time I did an apprenticeship and made countless pots. This wonderful experience honed my skills for building the ceramic form, and I dedicated myself to mastering design. I was crazy about clay. The surface was secondary.

Then the time came to set up my own studio and confront the considerable difficulties of making a living as a potter. Faced with limitations of space and finances, I "went electric," and bought an electric kiln. Because it was more economical, I switched to a lower temperature range for firing my work and sought ways to create painted and colorful surfaces. Suddenly, my world expanded.

I went on to study at Alfred University and Rutgers University, began a wholesale pottery business marketing through the American Crafts Council and American Craft Enterprises, and since then have been teaching at universities and colleges, art centers, and museums. I teach both beginning and advanced students the surface applications and techniques that may be used on low-fire ceramics. Working in low fire has now evolved into an exploration of the painterly pot as a means of self-expression.

I strive to find my own voice in my work, and I've always found individual expression inspiring in the work of others. For artists, the creative process is the same—it is the medium that changes. I encourage students to gain enough experience in application and technique to feel comfortable with ceramic technology. By gaining experience and mastering technique, they are freed to be self-expressive with the medium.

The methods in this book are ones that I have taught in my classes and workshops. I have taught people from all walks of life, from ages eight to 80, from those who had never seen clay before to those working on graduate degrees. Once introduced to surface decoration techniques, many students pursued the painted pot with passion.

Designing the piece is always the essence of surface decoration work. My students diligently design forms on paper before constructing their pieces. Without a sound form, the greatest decoration on earth will fall flat.

As experience increases, form and decoration tend to evolve together. Mastering the manufacturing technique is a big hurdle. However, when I think of the number of manufacturing techniques possible as compared with the vast combinations and possibilities for surface decoration, it is like comparing the amount of water in a teacup with the amount of water in the Atlantic Ocean.

I teach my students what I call the "coffee percolator school of art." Collect influences that you love and let them percolate and brew down until they become a blend that is your own personal expression. This handbook can be referred to at the rate that your exploration or needs demand. Experiment with the recipes and techniques. Keep notes of your processes and results. Combine things, break the rules, see what works for you, and—most of all—ENJOY!

Lynn Peters

In the Heat of the Kiln
Clay Basics and Getting Fired Up

It is also important to remember that, although pottery is made to be used, this fact in no way simplifies the problem of artistic expression; there can be no fullness or complete realization of utility without beauty, refinement and charm, for the simple reason that their absence must in the long run be intolerable to both maker and consumer. We desire not only food but also the enjoyment and zest of eating. The continued production of utilities without delight in making and using is bound to produce only boredom and to end in sterility.

—Bernard Leach, *A Potter's Book*

Surface decoration of ceramics is an art that demands knowledge of its materials and processes. Whether or not you're pleased with your piece when it leaves the kiln will be affected by the clay with which you built it, the surface applications with which you coated or painted it, the temperature at which you fired these interacting materials, and the length of the firing.

This book emphasizes materials and techniques for decorating the surface of your ceramic piece fired in what is referred to as the low-fire range of temperature. This is the range at which low-fire clay reaches maximum hardness or density. If you aren't familiar with temperature ranges for clay, you'll know more after you read this chapter. You'll also begin to understand the composition and nature of clay as well as stages of drying and firing. This introduction to these subjects will be helpful if you are a beginner (if you're an experienced potter, you might want to skip this section).

There are many books that can give you more technical information about clay, kilns, and firing. If you are totally uninitiated, and have never touched clay before, you might consider taking a class at your local university or art center. Getting your hands into the clay with the help of an experienced teacher can be one of the quickest routes to success.

THE CALL OF THE CLAY

When you encounter your first bag of clay it may be hard to imagine that this is the stuff that potters turn into everything from cozy teapots nestled on a kitchen shelf to architectural cornices perched high above a city street. The clay seems weighty, unyielding, cold, and (yikes!) damp.

Getting your hands into the clay changes that perception. After you open the bag, dig in, and start to warm it under the touch of your hands, it seems to immediately respond to your thoughts and ideas. You'll find that it is an exciting and sometimes unpredictable partner in the creative process. Learning the composition of clay and the way that it reacts to the drying process and to the heat of the kiln will cut out some of the guesswork for you. But always remember that much of the success of your work with the clay will come from your own repeated experiences with it. So don't be afraid to dig in and experiment!

CLAY BODIES AND OTHER MAGNIFICENT WONDERS

The clay that you use to make pots is for the most part composed of—you guessed it—clay. That slick, moist earth that you may have

Commercial clay bodies come bagged and ready to be used

slipped on as a kid is the same stuff that composes the foundation of all ceramics. Forming clay with your hands is as close to the earth, and as rudimentary and instinctual as any art form.

If you're talking to a geologist, he or she will refer to clay by its more formal name—*kaolinite*—which is a naturally occurring mineral created by the disintegration of feldspathic rock. Whatever the official name may be, remember that rudimentary clay is constantly underfoot.

The *plasticity* of clay, or its ability to readily change shape, holds it together and makes it usable for pottery. Test the plasticity of raw, unfired clay by rolling a small coil and wrapping it around your finger. If it doesn't crack, it may be pliable enough to use for pottery.

Potters alter naturally occurring clays by processing them with other materials. These mixtures of natural clay and other structurally compatible materials that make the clay workable and ideal for firing at certain temperatures are called *clay bodies*. Simply put, clay bodies are clays mixed for a particular use. Usually labeled as *earthenware*, *stoneware*, or *porcelain*, these blends have different compositions, which are determined by the heat at which they will harden and become nonporous, or *mature*, in the kiln. (With a commercial clay body, the label will suggest the temperature range at which the clay will mature.)

Changes in firing temperatures affect the shrinkage and color of the clay, and variations in ingredients affect the workability of the body. Some low-fire clay bodies, for instance, contain natural clays with a considerable amount of iron which causes them to fire at lower temperatures.

Many potters mix their own clay bodies, using any of the hundreds of recipes available from a variety of sources, including books on clay. Fortunately, for beginners and others who don't want to spend time on this process, commercial clay bodies come cleaned, prepared, and wrapped neatly in plastic bags from clay suppliers. The sticks and rocks have been removed and the clay has also been *pugged* (thoroughly mixed in a pug mill to eliminate the air bubbles) so that it can be used straight from the bag.

Your choice of clay body will always influence the final appearance of the surface of your piece, so it is wise to anticipate the type of surface treatment you will be giving the clay before you choose the body. Most clay suppliers will be happy to suggest a suitable one for the project you are planning. From that point, you'll still need to gain experience with each clay body, including how easy it is to handle, how much it shrinks, how well it accepts a glaze, how porous it is, and how its color changes after firing.

This book emphasizes work created with clay bodies fired at low temperatures—most often referred to as earthenware. The advantages of this type of clay body are many—including its availability, its minimal demand for fuel, and its ability to accommodate bright, colorful glazes. Given the great versatility of this clay, it's no surprise that low-fire work has gained prestige in the world of ceramics and art since the 1980s. Many potters now prefer to work solely with low-fire clay, when previously it was used primarily by industry and hobbyists.

STAGES OF CLAY DRYNESS

Clay, like any other substance, dries out when exposed to air. This happens when it's still in a plastic bag or container, waiting to be used, or being formed by the potter's hands.

When the clay is allowed to dry enough so that it doesn't retain finger marks but is still wet enough to be carved or joined, it's described as *leather hard*. Stiff leather-hard clay will crack if you try to bend it too far. (Clay should be covered lightly with plastic to prevent it from drying out too rapidly. Slow and even drying will help to prevent warping or cracking prior to firing in the kiln.)

Clay that has been slowly air-dried until it is as dry as possible prior to firing is aptly described as *bone dry*. Clay forms must be allowed to reach the bone-dry stage before they're fired in a kiln. At this stage of clay dryness the clay no longer feels cool to the touch, is extremely brittle and fragile, and must be handled carefully.

Any unfired clay object, whether leather hard or bone dry, is called *greenware*. Think of expressions such as "greenhorn" or "green as grass," and you'll have a quick way of remembering the meaning of greenware because the term describes pieces that are not yet mature or vitrified.

CLAY SHRINKAGE

Water is used to hold a clay body together for forming and will evaporate when the piece is left to dry. When this happens, the particles of the clay body move closer together, taking up the space left by the water. Then—you guessed it—the piece shrinks. The more plastic the clay, the more it may shrink, and consequently have a tendency to crack in the drying process. Adding materials with larger particles, such as grog, to the clay body, helps to prevent pieces from cracking while drying. The fact that clay shrinks when drying, as well as when exposed to the heat of the kiln, becomes especially relevant with certain surface decorations. The decoration and clay must *"fit"* each other—that is, they must shrink at similar rates or problems such as cracking and chipping can occur.

As you can see, clay bodies (as well as their coverings) are particular when it comes to the temperatures at which they will be cooperative. Fortunately, heat can be measured in a very simple manner in the kiln, which we'll investigate next.

CONES DEMYSTIFIED

For modern potters, testing kiln temperature is made more accurate through small, pyramid-shaped clay forms called *cones*. These are placed inside the kiln and formulated to bend and melt when the clay has reached its *maturation point*, or that at which it develops its maximum hardness and nonporosity. Potters are able to peek into the kiln's holes (wearing protective glasses) and see when the clay has reached the appropriate firing temperature.

Ranges of temperature are designated by a system of cone measurements. The seemingly cryptic language you'll run across such as "fired at cone 04" can easily be decoded with a standard chart of cone temperatures. This internationally used system simplifies temperature references for potters, and cones may be purchased that reflect this numbering system.

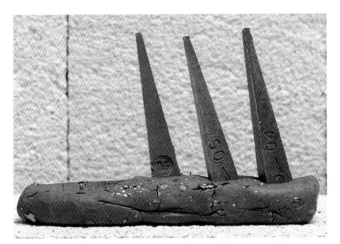

Potters test kiln temperature with small, pyramid-shaped cones.

Over the past few years, the computerized electric kiln has become the choice of many potters and schools. Rather than using cones that melt, the computer monitors the temperature and displays the cone temperature of the kiln on a digital screen. These kilns can be programmed by cone or temperature. Many potters prefer this method; others prefer being more involved with the process.

LOW-FIRE CLAY BODIES DEFINED

Potters often generalize about their works by referring to them as low-fire, mid-fire, or high-fire. As we've already learned, the type of clay that the potter uses dictates to a considerable extent the temperature at which any given piece is mature after being baked in the kiln. A low-fire clay body, for example, matures or "vitrifies" at relatively low temperatures; a high-fire clay body matures at much higher temperatures.

What temperature range is considered to be low-fire? Generally, low-fire commercial clay bodies begin to get hard but not mature at cone 015 (1479°F/804°C) and mature between cone 06 (1830°F/999°C) to cone 1 (2109°F/1154°C). Potters simplify these facts by referring to low-fire work as "fired at cone 06-01 range."

Materials used in low-fire clay bodies fall into four categories: clays; *fluxes* (substances that lower the melting point and consequently promote melting); *grogs* (materials with comparatively large particle sizes used to "open" a clay body and reduce shrinkage, cracking, and warping); and *colorants*. These components are combined to make the best clay body possible for a particular use. An example of a substance used in a low-fire clay body for a specific purpose is talc, a magnesium-bearing rock that acts as a flux and adds whiteness to the clay.

The most common low-fire pottery, earthenware, is created with the most readily available and profuse clay on earth. This clay is so common that it can be found in its raw state on the sides of highways, at construction sites, and even in backyards. Both earthenware and *terra cotta* (a type of earthenware) have been produced since ancient times. The Greeks made utilitarian earthenware pieces, and terra cotta was used by the Etruscans and other ancient peoples to create sculpture and ornamentation for buildings.

Several misconceptions exist about low-fire pottery. First, many people assume that low-fire clay bodies will not hold water, are soft, and will chip easily. In reality, the weaknesses just listed more often occur with high-fire stoneware clays that are fired at temperatures too low to allow the pieces to reach maturity. A low-fire clay body can vitrify at low temperatures, resulting in a dense, nonporous material. Second, the use of low-fire clay is not limited to the production of flower pots. It is now used to create very sophisticated contemporary ceramic pieces. Third, low-fire ware is sometimes viewed as a cheap imitation of porcelain, but this isn't true. There are actually very few true deposits of porcelain on earth, and most white clays that you see today are not porcelains but some variation of clays such as earthenware, terra cotta, or stoneware. When you first go to a clay supplier to purchase clay, you may be surprised at the number of variations of white earthenware clays available.

This gallery installation by Paul Sacaridiz uses painted terra-cotta pots to show number progressions.

Prior to firing, clays used to create earthenware and terra cotta range from red to gray. After firing, these clays may vary in appearance from white to dark brown. Low-fire clays have a wider color range than high-fire stonewares and porcelains and, unlike high-fire clays, they don't move or warp during firing. Because of these characteristics, it's easier to make a wide range of shapes and forms (large handles and flared rims, for example) in a broader color spectrum with low-fire clays.

It makes sense to choose a firing range and stick with it. Acquiring skill in a particular range requires an investment of time in trial and error but will ultimately save time. (For instance, if working in low-fire earthenware and high-fire stoneware, two or more separate firings of your pieces will be required because of differing temperature needs.)

The low-fire range is a great place to begin when learning ceramics. Because of its inherent versatility, this range is also a chosen destination for many of the most experienced and recognized ceramic artists in the world today.

SELECTING LOW-FIRE CLAY BODIES

You'll need to keep several things in mind when selecting a clay for low-fire work:

■ Select a clay body such as earthenware or terra cotta that is formulated for low-fire work. A "generic" clay body, with a wide firing range (cone 04-4, for example) can be used for low-fire as well as mid-fire ranges. But it's wiser to select low-fire clay with a narrow firing range, as close as possible to cone 04, so that the firing will bring the clay as close as possible to vitrification. The closer your low-fire clay is to vitrifying at cone 04, the tighter the clay body will be and the better the fit of the slip or glaze.

■ When selecting any clay body, including a low-fire one, consider plasticity in relationship to the type of construction techniques you'll be using. Hand-built pieces sometimes require different clay bodies than wheel-thrown pieces. If you're hand-building, for example, your clay body should contain a higher percentage of grog (fired clay which has been ground) to reduce shrinkage and warpage. For wheel-thrown work, a more plastic clay that will bend easily without cracking is needed in order to make tightly curved forms. (Again, it never hurts to ask your supplier for suggestions for a fit between the clay and your concept.)

■ Choose a clay that is compatible with the surface decoration materials that you plan to use.

For instance, decorations such as slips shrink during firing and must be matched to your selected clay body. (Slips and other decorations will be discussed in the coming pages.)

■ Remember that firing clay in a kiln changes the clay's color, and this may in turn affect your surface decoration colors if you are planning to allow certain areas of the clay to remain visible.

USING AN ELECTRIC KILN FOR LOW-FIRE WORK

When you're ready to change the clay from soft to hard, heat is required. No matter how much work you do beforehand, you have to eventually give up the clay to the kiln.

Ceramic kilns are differentiated by the fuel they use: electricity, gas, and wood are common kiln fuels. Each kiln has different capabilities. For low-fire surface decoration, electric kilns are the norm. Electric kilns have temperature limits that are somewhat lower than gas kilns and are usually used only for what is known as *oxidation firing*. Gas kilns, on the other hand, can reach very high temperatures and can be used for both oxidation and *reduction firing*.

What actually happens inside the kiln that distinguishes the oxidation process in an electric kiln from the reduction process of a gas kiln? An oxidizing atmosphere is one in which there is an ample supply of oxygen in the kiln chamber to guarantee that complete combustion of the contents occur. This is important not only for the clay, but for the glazes, because the oxidation-firing atmosphere contains enough oxygen to allow the production of bright colors.

In contrast, oxidation occurs in a gas or other reduction kiln through careful manipulation of the gas and oxygen ratio. A reduction atmosphere in the kiln reduces the proportion of gas to oxygen, forcing the oxygen-starved flame to attack the oxides in the clay and glazes of the ware. In other words, insufficient oxygen is supplied to the kiln for complete combustion and, instead, carbon monoxide in the kiln combines with oxygen in oxides of the clay body and glaze, causing them to change color. Such effects are associated with high-fire stoneware, porcelain, raku, and lusters. Creating inefficient combustion in the kiln is something potters do for aesthetic results—many believe that the colors are more beautiful when produced in this way.

Reduction firing isn't a natural process to undertake in an electric kiln because the air to fuel ratio in these kilns can't be manipulated; only electric elements are present for the conduction of heat. The only way to "reduce" in an electric kiln is to add carbon-yielding materials such as paper or sawdust to the kiln chamber, and these can damage the electric kiln elements.

Oxidation happens automatically in an electric kiln where there are only electric elements present for the conduction of heat, and therefore no air/fuel ratio to adjust. Low-fire glazes are conveniently fired in an electric kiln because they respond well to this environment and are associated with bright and clear colors fired in an oxidation atmosphere.

Working with low-fire clay and an electric kiln carries with it a host of advantages, some of which we've already discussed. First and fore-

Loading a glazed, decorated piece into an electric kiln

most is the ease and economic advantage of setting up a studio. Because low-fire work is most efficiently fired in an electric kiln, the artist is spared the expense and complication of plumbing, venting, chimney, and regulatory permits required by reduction kilns (such as gas, propane, wood, saw-dust, and oil-fired kilns). Less space is needed for electric kilns, and the materials needed for low-fire work, such as clay, slips, and glazes, are all available commercially.

Because low-fire work needs less heat and time to reach what potters call *vitrification* (or maturity), less fuel (in this case, electricity) is needed to obtain results. The potter is allowed to spend energy focusing on production. Many potters favor electric (or oxidation) kilns because of environmental concerns about fuel consumption and efficiency, and low-fire work causes less wear and tear on the kiln. Both the "hobby ceramics" industry and many school programs have benefited over the past 30 years from the technical advantages of the electric kiln.

STAGES OF FIRING: BISQUE AND GLAZE FIRING

Clay is usually fired in two stages: a *bisque firing* followed by a *glaze firing*. Bisque firing after the piece has reached the bone-dry stage hardens the clay and makes it easier to handle during glazing. Besides making the piece more stable, this firing releases trapped moisture from the clay that has not been released during drying. Superfluous organic materials in the clay are also burned out. The process of firing to the bisque stage should be done slowly to prevent steam from getting trapped, which can cause the piece to explode. Bisque firings usually peak between the relatively low temperatures of cone 08 and 010 so that the clay will not vitrify and will remain porous enough to absorb the glaze.

The glaze firing, which follows, melts the glazes, fusing them to the bisqued clay. (Gases that might otherwise have become trapped under the glaze were released during the bisque firing preventing pinholing.) Pieces may also be fired three or more times if overglazes are applied after glaze firing.

TESTING

Test Tiles

No matter what surface decoration you are applying, you should take the time to test the clay body and surface decoration material you plan to use with test tiles before making a kiln load of work.

Prepare test tiles by slicing several ¼"-inch-thick (0.6 cm or 6 mm) slabs of clay from your

Painting commercial underglaze colors onto a test tile

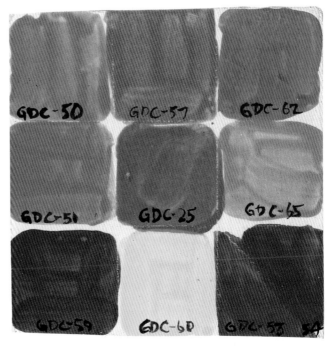

After the test tile has been fired and labeled with numbers indicating colors

block of premixed clay; then place them under loose sheets of plastic, and allow them to dry to the stage of dryness required for the work you are doing. You can also roll out a large slab of malleable clay and allow it to dry to almost leather hard, cut it into six-inch (15 cm) square tiles with a razor knife or pen tool, and make a hole in the center of the top edge of the tile for hanging later. Then proceed as you would with making a piece and apply any slips, under-glazes, glazes, or overglazes in consecutive firings. Always number or identify your test colors, whether commercial or studio-made.

Testing slips and glazes is one of the disciplines of ceramics. It's rather like exercising—it's an act that you may need to force yourself to do at first, and it may be frustrating and time consuming. Eventually, however, the benefits become apparent, and testing becomes a part of the everyday process.

A completed example of testing experimental images, marks, and techniques on a test tile

Journal

Creating a journal for your tests in a notebook with pages that you can remove and insert will prove invaluable as a learning tool. Record things such as your clay and glaze recipes, the application methods you use to create pieces, the stage of dryness of the clay when you apply each surface decoration, how long it took for a certain glaze to dry, the firing schedule for wares, reflections on the process—every step.

Think of keeping this journal as creating your own reference file, and include all the information you can gather. As with any form of research, documenting your process and results is critical. As the years go by, you won't remember specific details or procedures, but your journal will fill in any memory gaps. The journal will become your bible!

SAFETY

Coal miners no longer get silicosis of the lungs, potters are the ones who are now susceptible. Don't be scared, but do be cautious about your practices in the studio. Take precautions as a part of your routine, and you'll avoid problems.

Here are a few tips, but I also recommend reading the the two books by Monona Rossol listed at the end of this section.

■ Keep the floors and tables of your studio spotless by wiping them down often to avoid breathing dust from clays. Don't sweep—this can put clay dust back into the air. The best solution, if you're going to work with clay a lot, is the addition of a professionally installed ventilation system to filter out dust.

■ Set up your kiln outside or have it vented outside with its own local exhaust system. The fumes from kilns are bad for you, which will be obvious when you first smell them. Sulfur dioxide, carbon monoxide, hydrogen chloride, and nitrogen oxide are but a few of the gases emitted. Luster glazes are the worst carcinogens, and I don't recommend using them for this reason. Eliminate using wax as a resist for glazing since it is toxic when it burns off in the kiln.

■ Wear a respirator whenever you do anything with dry clay, glaze, or plaster. Make certain you have it fitted correctly to your face. If you have a beard or wear glasses, a respirator won't work.

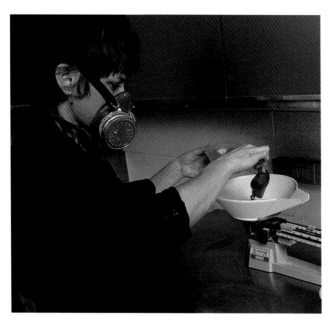

Wear a respirator when working with dry ingredients.

■ Always use welder's glasses when looking into a peephole of a kiln. You need to protect yourself from ultraviolet rays as well as anything that might fly out of the kiln and hit you in the eye.

■ Change and launder your clothing, apron, and shoes frequently. Wearing an apron that is crusty with clay is putting you at risk of breathing more clay dust. Remove your dirty garments before entering your living environment. Wash your hands frequently using a fingernail brush. If using stains, wash your hands often or wear surgical gloves to keep them from getting into your bloodstream.

■ Wear surgical gloves when mixing colors and glazing. If using commercial products, always read the labels. Formulas often change without notification. Be aware of what you are using and any dangers that might be listed on the label.

■ Label every material you have in your studio, noting its toxicity.

■ When buying commercial glazes and under-glazes for use on dinnerware, check the labels to make sure they're safe for this purpose.

■ If you are pregnant, don't work with clay. Supervise children closely if they are working with you on clay projects.

■ Never leave flammable materials such as wood, clothing, or paper close to a hot kiln.

■ Keep a fire extinguisher nearby, especially if you use an oil-fired kiln. Fire is less of a danger with an electric kiln, but, if using one, an extinguisher should still be part of your equipment in the studio. Never put out a fire with water, use sand or an extinguisher instead.

Two great sources of information related to studio safety, both written by Monona Rossol, are *The Artist's Complete Health and Safety Guide*, 2nd. ed. (New York: Allworth Press, 1994) and *Keeping Clay Work Safe and Legal* (Bandon, Oregon: National Council on Education for the Ceramic Arts, 1996). Ms. Rossol provides understandable and accurate information on health hazards faced by ceramicists and how to prevent them.

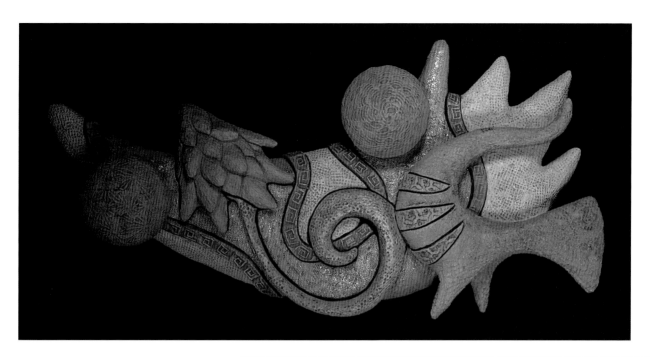

▲ **BRYAN HIVELY** (Cook, Minnesota), *Habitat Progression*, 31 x 20 x 8" (77.5 x 50 x 20 cm), 1997. Earthenware. Handbuilt using coils. Underglazes, slips, textured glazes. Δ04 firing.
Photo by Anne Boudreau.

▶ **ANDREA GILL** (Alfred, New York), *Ripe Pods*, 44 x 27 x 12" (110 x 67.5 x 30 cm), 1996. Low-fire terra cotta. Slab built using pressmolds and handbuilding. Colored slips, stencilling. Clear glaze spattered on surface with toothbrush before firing. Δ03 firing and Δ07 bisque firing.

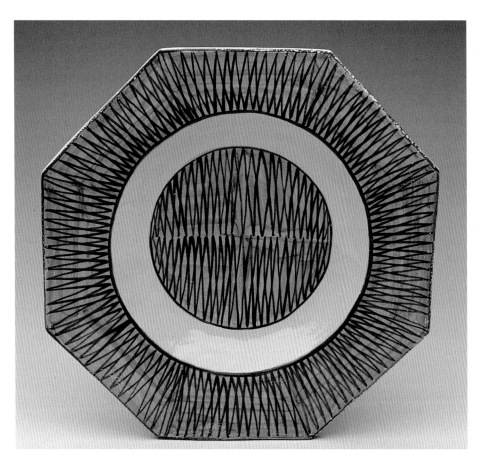

◀ **LYNN PETERS** (Lynn Peters (Chicago, Illinois), ***Charger***, 20" diameter (50 cm), 1997. Maiolica. Δ04 firing.
Photo by Jeff Martin.

▼ **CAROLYN GENDERS** (West Sussex, Great Britain), ***Bowls***, 4 x 12", 2.4 x 36" (10 x 30 cm, 6 x 15 cm), 1996. White earthenware. Wheel thrown. Sponged and painted engobes, wax resist, sgraffito. Clear glaze and luster. Δ02 firing.
Photo by artist.

▲ **MICHEL LOUISE CONROY**
(San Marcos, Texas), ***Vase from
Stir/Still Series***, 15.5 x 6.5 x
6.5" (39 x 16.3 x 16.3 cm),
1992. White earthenware.
Wheel thrown using coil and
throw method. Slips in multiple
layers. Clear glaze. Δ04 bisque
firing. Δ06 glaze firing.
Photo by artist.

▲ **MITCH YUNG** (Branson,
Missouri), ***Twist Buffet Platter***,
25 x 9.5 x 2.25" (62.5 x 23.8 x
5.6 cm), 1998. Red earthenware.
Handbuilt, slab construction, bas
relief carving. Terra sigillata. Δ04
firing. Photo by Rockafellow Photography.

◄ **MELODY ELLIS** (Philadelphia, Pennsylvania), *Harvest Tile*, 5 x 5 x .5" (12.5 x 12.5 x 1.3 cm), 1997. Terra cotta. Image drawn on surface and negative areas carved away at leather-hard stage. Δ04 firing. Sealed after fired, recesses filled with black grout. Photo by artist.

▲ **CARY ESSER** (Kansas City, Missouri), *Sarracenia Leaf*, 8 x 8 x 1" (20 x 20 x 2.5 cm), 1996. Red earthenware. Press mold. Bas relief. Terra sigillata applied to unfired clay. Glazes applied to bisque. Δ04 firing. Photo by Seth Tice-Lewis.

◄ **MICHEL LOUISE CONROY** (San Marcos, Texas), *Teapot*, 17.5 x 6 x 10.5" (43.8 x 15 x 26.3 cm), 1995. White earthenware. Wheel thrown, neck added using coil and throw method. Pulled handle and foot. Sgraffito used at leather-hard stage and brushed with slips in layers. Δ04 bisque firing. Δ06 glaze firing. Photo by artist.

▲ **DEBORAH BLACK** (Toronto, Canada), *Coral Teapot*, 7 x 13 x 3" (17.5 x 32.5 x 7.5 cm), 1998. Red earthenware. Handbuilt with slabs. Slips, glazes. Δ04 firing.

▶ **ERIK JOHANSON** (Tinton Falls, New Jersey), *Entwined*, 10.5 x 7.5 x 7" (26.3 x 18.8 x 17.5 cm), 1997. Red earthenware. Slab-formed cylinder, finger pressed, closed with small slabs at top, coils at bottom. Carved and burnished ridges, brushed with three coats red terra sigillata, burnished between coats. Δ08 firing.
Photo by Jeff Martin.

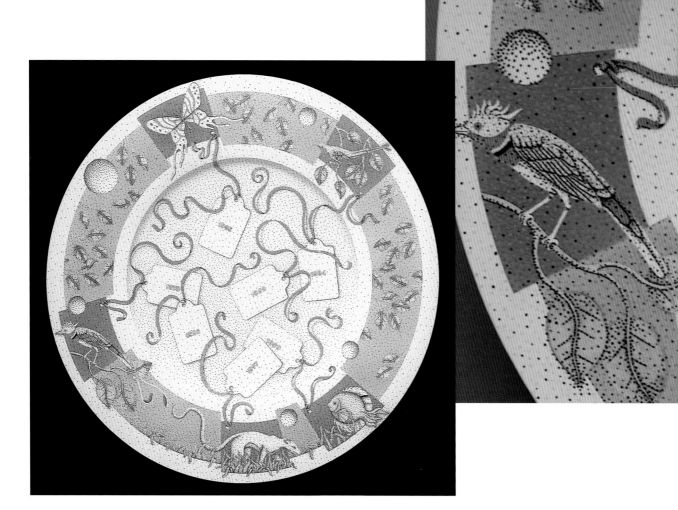

▲ **STEPHEN PATT** (Aguanga, California), *Tagged,* 22" diameter (55 cm), 1989. Porcelain. Masked, airbrushed, and stippled underglaze and underglaze pencil. Clear glaze. Δ5 bisque firing. Δ05-06 glaze firing. Photo by Michael Easley.

▶ **ANNE KRAUS** (Boulder, Colorado), *Teapot,* 8 x 6.5" (20 x 16.3 cm), 1989. Whiteware. Slips, underglazes. Courtesy of Garth Clark Gallery, NYC.

▶ **MARSHA McCARTHY**
(Holliston, Massachusetts),
Precious Child, 16 x 20"
(40 x 50 cm), 1997.
Earthenware. Slip cast mold.
Sgraffito. Δ04 firing.

▼ **LYNN PETERS** (Chicago,
Illinois), ***Vases***, 6-18" height (15-
45 cm), 1997. Red earthen-
ware. Slip cast. Slips, glaze.
Sgraffito. Δ04 firing.
Photo by Jeff Martin.

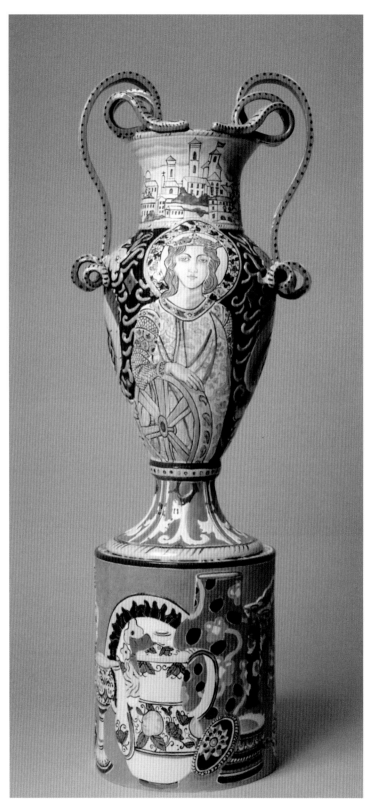

▲ **ANNE FARLEY GAINES**
(Chicago, Illinois), *Sister
Mermaids*, 1998. 17 x 6.5"
(42.5 x 16.25 cm), Coil built.
Underglaze decoration. Δ04 firing.

▲ **KAREN KOBLITZ** (Los Angeles,
California), *Santa Caterina of Deruta*,
24.75 x 8.5 x 8.5" (62 x 21.3 x 21.3 cm),
1997. White earthenware. Thrown vase
and pedestal, slab handles. Surface carving
and underglazes applied at greenware
stage. Matte and gloss glazes after bisque
firing. Δ04 bisque firing. Δ06 glaze firing.
Photo by Susan Einstein.

▶ **WILLIAM BROUILLARD**
(Cleveland, Ohio), *Top Hat*,
5 x 24 x 24" (12.5 x 60 x 60
cm), 1995. Red earthenware.
Molded and wheel thrown.
Maiolica glaze with painted
glaze stain. Δ05 firing.

▶ **CHUCK AYDLETT** (St. Cloud,
Minnesota), *Care*, 12 x 13 x 8"
(30 x 32.5 x 20 cm), 1994.
Earthenware. Handbuilt.
Maiolica. Δ04 firing. Courtesy of
Ferrin Gallery, Northhampton, MA.

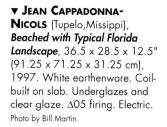

◀ **SUSAN PAPA** (Midlothian, Virginia), **Untitled**, 9 x 10 x 6" (22.5 x 25 x 15 cm), 1998. Red earthenware. Slab-built body and arms. Sgraffito on body. Extruded coils at base and neck. Carved and underglazed coils. Waxed exterior. Δ04 firing.

Photo by Eric Norbom.

▼ **JEAN CAPPADONNA-NICOLS** (Tupelo, Missippi), *Beached with Typical Florida Landscape*, 36.5 x 28.5 x 12.5" (91.25 x 71.25 x 31.25 cm), 1997. White earthenware. Coil-built on slab. Underglazes and clear glaze. Δ05 firing. Electric.

Photo by Bill Martin.

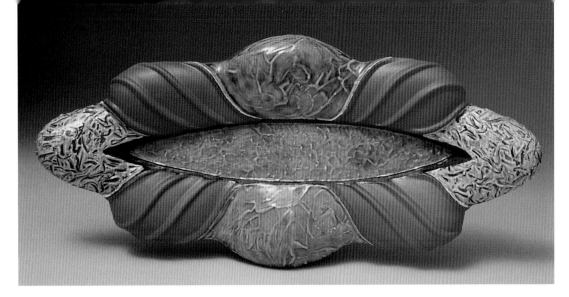

▲ **Mark Johnson** (South Portland, Maine), *Long Platter*, 3 x 18 x12" (7.5 x 45 x 30 cm), 1997. Red earthenware. Formed in a plaster slump mold. Foot coil added. Terra sigillata and black cracking slip. Δ04 firing.
Photo by artist.

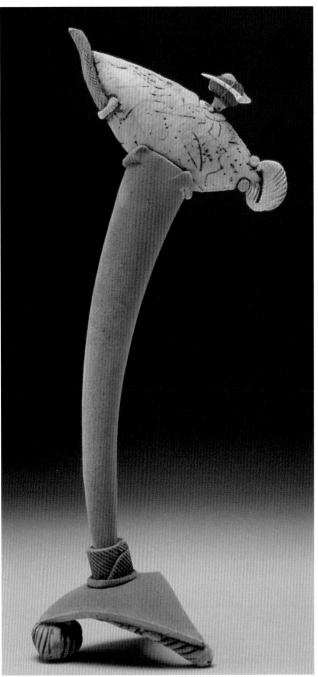

▲ **Lisa Woollam** (Ontario, Canada), *Platter*, 2.4 x 11.8 x 11.6" (6 x 29.5 x 29 cm),1998. Red earthenware. Press mold, carved when leather hard. Terra sigillata, maiolica, sgraffito. Δ06 bisque firing. Δ05 glaze firing.
Photo by artist.

▶ **Kathy Triplett** (Weaverville, North Carolina), *Colors Tea*, 24 x 11 x 10" (60 x 27.5 x 25 cm), 1998. White earthenware. Slab and extruded. Stains and underglazes, sprayed glazes. Δ05 firing. Photo by Tim Barnwell

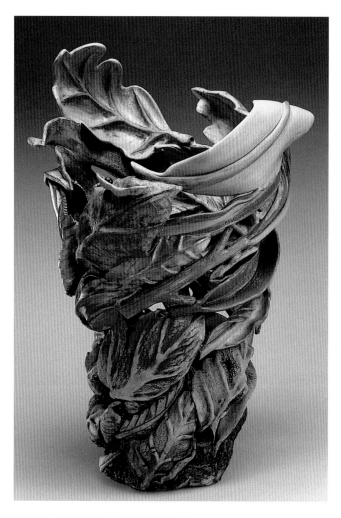

◄ **LINDA HUEY** (Alfred Station, New York), *Wind*, 28 x 18 x 18" (70 x 45 x 45 cm), 1998. Handbuilt. Colored glazes. Δ04 firing. Photo by Brian Oglesbee.

▼ **GAIL KENDALL** (Lincoln, Nebraska), *Tureen*, 10 x 17.5 x 8" (25 x 43.8 x 20 cm), 1998. Terra cotta. Coiled, scraped, and paddled. White slip, underglazes, colored transparent glazes. Δ07 bisque firing. Δ04 glaze firing. Photo by artist.

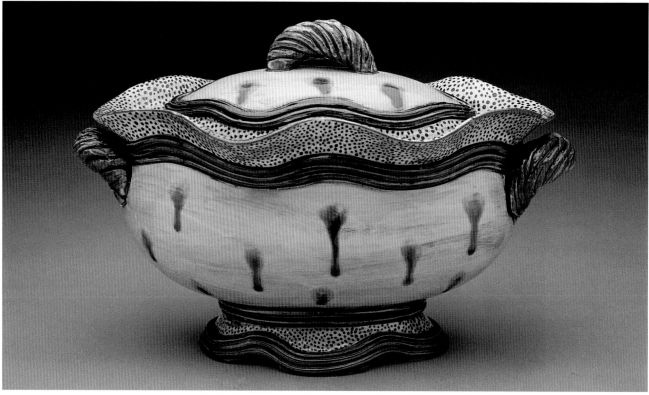

▲ **Lisa Orr** (Austin, Texas), *Teapot, Cup, and Saucer*, 7 x 8.5 x 6", 4 x 5.5 x 5.5" (17.5 x 21.3 x 15 cm, 10 x 13.8 x 13.8 cm), 1998. Earthenware. Wheel thrown. Sprigged clay. Terra sigillata, slips, glazes. Δ03 firing.

▶ **Lisa M. Naples** (Doylestown, Pennsylvania), *Soup Tureen*, 11 x 16 x 14" (27.5 x 40 x 35 cm), 1997. Earthenware. Handbuilt with slabs. Slips, transparent and colored glazes. Δ04 firing.

COLOR, FORM, AND LINE
Surface Applications and Techniques

Thorough discipline gives the skills needed to enable freedom of expression so that one is not bound up with the "how-to," and can concern oneself with the "why-to." It is like the musician who practices endless scales and arpeggios, without which he cannot make music. If we are to "make music" in our clay works, an understanding of form, details, and variations is our equivalent of the musician's scales and arpeggios. Without them our compositions are amorphous and limp.

-Robin Hopper, from *A Potter's Companion: Imagination, Originality, and Craft* by Ronald Larson

An exciting array of applications is available for decorating the surfaces of ceramic pieces. This chapter will introduce you to a series of these applications, such as slips, underglazes, and overglazes. Techniques for using them, including brushing, sgraffito, and slip trailing, will also be discussed. Because surface applications are composed of materials that react to drying and the heat of the kiln in certain ways, they serve different purposes, and each is usually layered on the the piece in a specific order. This does not mean that potters don't experiment and break the rules to achieve new effects. But, for our purposes, we'll concentrate on what is more "tried and true," and that which is often taught in studio classrooms.

At first the subject of surface decoration may seem complex, especially if you look at a finished piece and try to decipher all the steps that were taken without first working through this information. But after exploring this subject with patience, you'll begin to recognize how each layer of application is created and why. Not only that, but you'll develop a desire to take up a paintbrush, a sgraffito tool, or a stencil and launch your own discovery or rediscovery of low-fire surface treatments. Then your knowledge will be further reinforced by seeing step-by-step photos in Chapter Three of the applications being used.

Slips

Slips are finely sieved mixtures of clay and water, either white or colored, which can be applied to clay surfaces in one or more layers. They are applied to create a neutral ground on which to apply surface decorations, and they can also be painted on as colored decorations. Slips create a matt effect on the pottery's surface until glaze fired. Recipes for slips—each formulated to dry, shrink, and be fired in relationship to a specific clay body—are available in many pottery books. The recipe will tell you the temperature at which the particular slip will vitrify and will help you match it with the proper clay body.

With slips, what you see is what you get. Because they don't melt or soften during firing, slips don't run, fade, blur, or combine with other slips as do glazes (which we'll investigate later). Every brush mark and decorative element that you create with the slip remains exactly the same after firing the clay—this also means that every fingerprint and imperfect area of your slip decoration will show up after firing. The results are predictable, controllable, and can be traced to your experimentation and test journal.

Slips colored in the studio with mixtures of oxides or ceramic stains are a favorite of potters for surface decoration. Oxides and carbonates such as copper, cobalt, or manganese, all of which are available from ceramic suppliers and come in powdered form, are chemical compounds that act as coloring agents in clay, slips, and glazes. Cobalt oxide, for example, turns clay blue, and copper oxide yields green. Stains, which come in a wider variety of colors than oxides, are commercially prepared combinations of ingredients that may be incorporated into clay or clay slip to color it. Stains may also be added in small amounts to glazes.

Most studio-produced colored slips are formulated for application to clay in the leather-hard greenware state. If applied to compatible leather-hard clay, the clay body and slip will shrink at the same rate, creating a good fit between clay and decoration. You'll find tips for application of slip to greenware in the following section.

Once applied, a slip (like any clay substance) must be allowed to dry before it is fired in the kiln. (As with other surface decorations, it is always a good idea to then fire the slip on a test tile before investing huge amounts of time and materials on finished pieces.)

Slips that are formulated for bisqued clay are less common because the slip has more of a tendency to shrink on prefired clay. Sometimes this problem can be solved by thinning the slip consistency. Also, you'll find that some slip recipes are specifically formulated for use on bisqued clay.

Through years of teaching, hundreds of my students and I have used the following slip recipe with a host of clay bodies. It's nicknamed "Old Reliable" because it has a wide range of fit for various clays, even when the clay comes straight from someone's backyard.

Old Reliable Slip Recipe/cone 06-03

I think of this as the "all-forgiving slip." I believe that this white slip recipe originally came from Alfred University, in Alfred, New York.

Old Mine #4/Kentucky Ball clay	40 g
Edgar's Plastic Kaolin	20 g
Nepheline Syenite (flux)	10 g
Talc	15 g
Flint	15 g

This formula adds up to 100 grams. (Most ceramic recipes are given in measurements that add up to 100 grams.) If planning to add colorants to the slip, you'll need to make a few thousand grams at one time and then divide it up so that you can add colorants to each portion. To mix 1000 grams, just multiply the quantities of each ingredient by 10 so that your recipe looks like this:

Old Mine #4/Kentucky Ball clay	400 g
Edgar's Plastic Kaolin	200 g
Nepheline Syenite	100 g
Talc	150 g
Flint	150 g

Steps for mixing:

1. Begin by putting on a good respirator and a pair of plastic gloves. Use a triple beam balance scale to measure out each of the dry ingredients in the quantity indicated in the formula. (Subtract the weight of the container you use to measure the ingredients from the weight of the dry ingredients after you weigh them.) Set each dry ingredient aside as you weigh it.

2. Next, estimate how much space your combined dry ingredients will take in a five-gallon (19.2 L) bucket in which you'll be mixing them. (Approximately 10,000 grams of dry weight will fill half of a five-gallon bucket.) Then, measure out slightly less water than half the volume of your dry ingredients and pour it into the empty bucket first. If the dry ingredients would fill half the bucket, for example, fill a little less than one-quarter of the bucket with water. This method will help you avoid ending up with slip that is too runny—you can always add more water to the slip later as you're mixing in the dry ingredients.

3. Add your already-measured dry ingredients to the water, folding them in to wet them, just as if you were mixing pancakes. Then, mix thoroughly using a mixer blade attached to an electric drill (you can get this at a hardware store because it's often used to mix paint). Ideally, a well-mixed slip should be about the same consistency as cream. The slip is too thick if it is the consistency of yogurt. Once you've tested your slip, you may want to experiment with the consistency of future batches, testing each one and adjusting it as necessary for the thickness and moisture levels of your clay and for your particular touch during application.

4. After mixing the slip as described above, you should sieve the mixture through a 30-mesh screen into a clean container.

Mixing Slip with Colorants

To make colored slips, you'll need to add colorants to the dry ingredients before adding water. To color my slips, I almost always use stains because they provide strong colors. They're also reliable, predictable, and surprise proof. (A variety of colors of stain may be purchased at ceramic supply stores.) Stains must be added to slips in order to fire onto the piece permanently without a sealing glaze.

Instead of adding the dry ingredients to water as we did with the white slip mixture, you'll be making what is called a "dry mix" first. Mix the dry ingredients from the slip recipe together thoroughly in a bucket. Then divide the mixture into five equal portions and place each into a clean bucket. This proportion makes a convenient measurement, because each portion will then be around 200 grams.

To calculate how much stain to use, figure 15% of the weight of the dry ingredients in the bucket and add that amount of stain to the slip. For instance, if each bucket holds 200 grams of dry ingredients, you'll add 15% of 200, or 30 grams of stain. (If you'd rather color your slip with oxides, see Appendix IX for a list of oxides and proportions in which to add them.)

A collection of various colors of stains for coloring slips or overglazes

Next mix the colorants that you've chosen into each bucket of dry ingredients. With 200 grams of dry mix, you should begin mixing with approximately one cup (240 mL) of water. Add the dry ingredients to the water and stir—if you need more water, add more at that point. When it's the consistency of cream, it's ready. Sieve the colored slip through a 30-mesh screen into clean containers (such as yogurt tubs) that can be tightly sealed. Label each container as well as its lid, so the same lid always goes back on each one. You'll save a lot of confusion later if you do this right after mixing.

Always be sure to stir slips well (don't shake) before applying them to clay. Use a clean area, free of debris and dirt, to mix and use slips so that you don't contaminate them. Don't dilute them with water unless really needed—it's difficult to reconstitute the mixture once it's too thin.

Keep the following things in mind when applying slips:

▪ Slips can be used on bisqueware, but I prefer to use them on greenware because there seems to be a more natural fit between the clay and the slip before firing. After experimenting with slips on both greenware and bisqueware, you'll find your own preference.

▪ Realize that the drying time of a slip application varies. The drier the clay the slip is applied to, the faster the slip will dry. A slip applied to wet or damp leather-hard clay will naturally take longer to dry than one applied to a bone-dry or bisqued surface. Differences in drying times can also be caused by variations in the thickness of the walls of your pieces or an air draft in your working area. However, variations in drying time won't effect the final look of the piece.

▪ Slips may be applied with a variety of tools including a brush, a spraygun, a sponge, or a palette knife. You can also dip or pour slips to cover the surface. Always be aware that the tool that you choose will affect the thickness of the

Applying a coat of slip to greenware using a wide hakeme brush

slip. Thick applications of slip (which contain more moisture than thin ones) will dry more slowly. For example, *slip trailing*, which means applying the slip with a squeeze bottle or other nozzle) can give you a thick application. If your slip starts to lift off after it dries, it is probably too thick and you need to squeeze out a finer line. To help prevent this problem, practice with wet slip on newspaper to see how a line looks before you try it on your piece.

▪ Applying several coats of slip will uniformly color your whole piece since slip has an opaque quality. It is possible to paint multiple coats of slip on greenware over the course of weeks if you wrap the clay you're working on in airtight plastic between work sessions. Doing this will keep the clay from drying out over time.

Applying Slip to Greenware and Bisqueware

As we've already discussed, the best stage of dryness for applying slip to clay is when it is leather hard. However, if the clay is too wet, or not dried at all, it will sag or melt with the added moisture of the wet slip application. To be certain that it has reached the leather-hard stage, you should be able to handle it carefully without leaving indentations with your fingers. Although the clay will still hold the imprint of a fingernail, simple handling shouldn't distort it.

To test slips on leather-hard greenware you'll need to prepare several clay test tiles and allow them to dry to the leather-hard stage. (Slips for bone-dry greenware and bisqueware should be tested on bone-dry and bisque-fired tiles.)

A completed example of testing slips and techniques on a test tile

After painting on the slip and allowing it to dry you will know if it is right for your particular clay body. If it fits and doesn't peel off or crack, then it will probably work. If it is going to crack, it will usually happen in the drying process, which usually means that the slip is too thick. Thinning it with water may do the trick.

The safest and cleanest way to add any form of decoration to your piece, including slip, is to place the piece on a turntable such as a circular *banding wheel* or a revolving stand—similar to a "lazy Susan"—which sculptors and ceramicists use to slowly turn work. You can then move the piece by revolving the circular base of the stand and not touching the clay. This will reduce your need to handle the piece. If you must handle it while painting on the slip, you will be likely to leave fingerprints or smears on it. To prevent smearing of the slip, you can also turn your piece while applying slips by holding it upside down with your hand supporting it inside (if its

shape allows). Naturally, you'll need to paint the outside first before the inside if doing this.

Natural air currents in your studio will dry out the clay while you're working on it. To keep your piece moist, mist your leather-hard surface with water from an atomizer spray bottle as needed while you're working. If completing the piece in stages, cover it with a sheet of plastic to keep it from drying out between sessions.

You should be prepared to leave 10- to 20-minute intervals between each layer of applied slip so that each can become leather hard before the next layer is applied. This is a good time to evaluate what you've painted so far, and plan for the next part of your design.

You can apply slip to bisqueware using the same recipe that we used earlier for greenware. Simply add water to the Old Reliable Slip recipe—whether white or colored—until it thins to about three-quarters of its original thickness, or the consistency of cream. Slip applied to bisqueware will dry almost instantly because of the absorption factor of the dry clay.

TERRA SIGILLATA

Terra sigillata, or "terra sig" as it is fondly called, is another variety of slip. The original use of the phrase described certain Roman pressed or embossed ware: *terra* (earth) and *sigil* (seal or stamp). Later it came to denote Greek and Roman earthenware decorated with an unglazed, shiny surface. Well-known examples of terra sig can be seen in glossy red and black Greek vases and the glowing red of Roman figure-ware vases from as early as the seventh century B.C. Today, it is used to produce a broader range of effects.

In the process of creating terra sig, the larger particles of clay are separated out so that only the finest particles of micalike clay remain. Like other slips, terra sig appeals to those who prefer the effect that is lent by the decoration becoming an integral part of the clay body.

Terra sig is made by mixing a fine clay with water and water softener (a *deflocculant* which thins the mixture), then allowing it to settle for 24 hours. The coarse particles settle to the bottom, leaving a layer of water on top, a layer containing fine particles in the middle, and the coarse particles on the bottom. After being siphoned off, only the middle layer is applied in thin coats to dry, unfired ware.

Terra sig can be brushed, sponged, sprayed, dipped, or poured in a very thin coat on bone-dry greenware—the stage of clay dryness at which it most readily adheres. The application will be watery because it is considerably thinner than regular slips. Like other slips, terra sig is not normally applied to fired bisqueware, but rather to bone-dry greenware, since the simple clay ingredients are less likely to "fit" most clay bodies if applied after the preliminary firing.

This slip-like painting medium dries to a soft, silky sheen unless fired at too high of temperature. Although terra sig doesn't create a hard seal as would a typical glaze, it helps to seal the clay surface and make it somewhat impervious to water. If painted on and fired without a glaze, terra sig creates a matte surface which cannot be used on functional objects which must hold water, but which can be used for decorative purposes. Nonporous, foodsafe ware can be created through the use of a protective glaze fired on top of terra sig.

Terra sig is an accessible way to enhance the surface of your clay body, and can be painted on as a decoration as well as juxtaposed with colorful glazed areas to create dramatic contrasts. It is often used in combination with other applications, but can stand on its own as a powerful surface decoration.

Terra Sigillata Recipe/cone 06-03

The following red terra sig recipe is straightforward and easy to use. I use it with my students.

> 3 cups (720 mL) water (distilled if possible)
> 400 g fine-grained earthenware clay
>   (Red Art works well)
> 3-7 drops of Darvon #7
>   (or sodium silicate deflocculant)

Pour water into a clear tall container that will hold at least two quarts (1.92 L). A plastic soda bottle with the neck cut off works well. Measure and add the clay to the water in increments and mix thoroughly. A kitchen blender or a drill with a mixer attachment on the end are helpful for mixing the ingredients.

Slowly drop in three or four drops of deflocculant while carefully stirring the mixture until you see it visibly thinning out to the consistency of homogenized milk. Don't add more deflocculant than you need, or the mixture will begin to thicken instead of thinning. Then you'll have to start over.

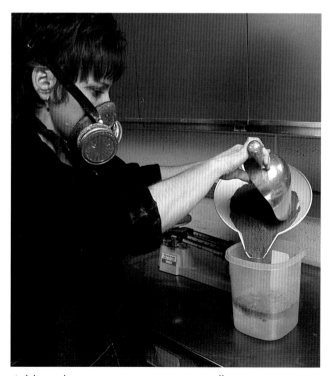

Adding clay to water to mix terra sigillata

After thinning, continue mixing the ingredients for five minutes. Let it settle for 24-48 hours.

After a day, you'll see three layers in your container:

1. The top layer will be water. Siphon or decant it off without disturbing the settled clay. Discard it.

2. The middle layer will contain the finest clay particles, or the terra sig. Carefully siphon or decant this layer into a plastic container. Cover it with plastic wrap or seal it before labeling it. You can use the terra sig right away, but stir it with every use it because it settles quickly.

3. The bottom layer contains large-particled left overs. Discard this layer.

Settled layers of terra sigillata before decanting

Using a Studio-Made Clay Body to Make Terra Sigillata

You may also use a studio-made earthenware clay body (such as the one listed in Appendix I) to make a terra sig. Or you can experiment with clay deposits that you find in nature—the red or ochre-colored earths you come across in your travels or in your backyard may provide you with a rich terra sig. In order to use these kinds of clay from nature, you must always first sieve the clay through a screen (I recommend 100-mesh for this purpose) to remove large particles. A clay body that contains a lot of grog will defeat your purpose of making a fine-particled application. Because the clay that you might choose to make your own terra sig hasn't been commercially tested, you'll always have to test it first with the clay body that you're firing it on.

To do this, allow a few pounds (3 lbs = 1.4 kg) of clay to dry to the bone-dry stage. Then cover the clay with enough water to submerge it in a gallon bucket or larger. Leave it overnight to combine until it reaches the consistency of yogurt (potters call this process *slaking*). In a blender or with a drill fitted with a mixer attachment, mix the clay with water for ten minutes. Water should be added until it becomes the consistency of heavy cream. Then, continue to mix it and add drops of deflocculant until it visibly thins to the consistency of milk. Now pour it into a clear container such as a soda bottle and wait for the layers to separate. Decant the layers as explained above in the terra sig recipe.

Adding Colorants to Terra Sigillata

Most natural terra sigillata will fire from red to brown in an oxidation kiln atmosphere and black in a reduction kiln atmosphere. If planning to color terra sig, you'll need to use a white terra sig so that the color will show. For a good place to start, follow the recipe below, using the same instructions that you used for the red terra sig recipe on page 37.

White Terra Sigillata Recipe

> 3 cups (720 mL) water
> 400 g Old Mine # 4 Ball clay
> 3-7 drops of Darvon # 7
>   (or sodium silicate deflocculant)

You can color white terra sig by adding colorants in the form of oxides or stains that you select from color charts at a ceramic supplier. Add 5% to 15% of the stain to the dry clay before stirring it into the water and adding the deflocculant. In other words, the dried colorants will become a part of your terra sig formula—you're just adding another ingredient. (If you'd rather color your terra sig with oxides, see Appendix IX for a list of oxides and proportions in which to add them.) If the surface of the terra sig appears dull after firing, you may have added too much colorant.

Use a 30-mesh screen for sieving the colorants into the mix to avoid intense bursts of color. Always test colored terra sigs first by firing on a tile. The process will be similar to testing slips.

Using Terra Sigillata in Combination with Glazes

Terra sig can be used in combination with other glazes for interesting surface effects. Terra sig is especially beautiful in combination with a contrasting glaze, such as maiolica. (We'll cover glazes and maiolica later in this chapter.)

To do this, begin with a piece that you've allowed to dry to the leather-hard stage. Paint terra sig on the sections of your piece where you don't plan to apply the glaze, and let it dry about 15 minutes. Next, bisque fire the piece. After firing, use liquid wax from a ceramic supply store— melting your own wax can be a fire hazard—to paint over the terra sig decoration and prevent it from receiving glazed. (The wax will melt off in the kiln later.) After applying other glazes, fire the piece again. The areas that you covered with terra sig will make a nice contrast to maiolica or brightly colored glazes.

UNDERGLAZES

Underglazes can be defined broadly as any coloring material used under a glaze. This term is now commonly used for commercially made products colored with oxides and stains formulated to color greenware and bisqueware before glaze is applied. These underglazes are the commercial, prepackaged equivalent of studio-made slips that have been colored. Most beginning and many advanced potters prefer to buy commercial underglazes because they are so accessible, while other potters like to make their own colored slips to be used at the underglaze stage of decoration. After decorating with slips and underglazes, the piece is sealed with a clear glossy glaze to bring out the full intensity of the underglazes' colors and seal them to the clay.

To remember the basics about slips and underglazes it helps to think of them as liquid clay. This will help you differentiate them from glazes, which fire to a glasslike surface instead of the matt surface of slips and underglazes.

Commercially produced products for decoration: chalks, pencils, markers, semi-moist pan colors, and jars of liquid color

You might ask why you couldn't put stains or colorants into a clear glaze and use it as an underglaze. The answer will again help you remember the difference between the two. If stains or colorants are added to clear glaze the colorants flow with the melting glaze and move around on the surface of the piece. The purpose of underglazes is to adhere and stay where placed so that brush stroke painting and outlines are possible. They are often compared to watercolors in their effect, especially if painted on bisqueware, which provides a highly absorbent surface akin to heavy paper.

Surface decorations created with underglazes tend to be quite durable after they are fired under a protective glaze. Because of their chemical composition, underglazes will hold fast to the clay surface without being blurred by overcoats of glazes fired on top of them. There is no chance of an underglaze running off the piece during firing. Because of this, they can be used to create depth through layers.

Instant Gratification: Commercial Underglazes

Commercial, ready-made underglazes are the quickest form of instant gratification for potters. While these products were first designed for the "hobbyist," many professional artists use such commercial products for their constancy, reliability, availability, and predictability.

Commercial underglazes are carefully composed liquid mixtures of the following: ceramic stains, for color; fluxes, which lower the melting point; refractory materials, which resist heat; and binders, which hold it all together.

Application techniques that use studio-made slips can also be undertaken with commercial underglaze products. (Surface decoration techniques are demonstrated with both studio-made slips and commercial products in Chapter Three.) Some potters choose to use studio-made and commercial products in combination on the same piece. Commercial underglazes can be used on both greenware

and bisqueware and are sold in a variety of forms, including chalks, crayons, and pencils as well as tubes or pans.

Sharpening underglaze pencils with an exacto blade and sandpaper

Commercial underglazes need to be tested with your clay body like any slip. They work best when applied to bone-dry greenware or bisqueware, but can be applied at any stage during the processes of drying and firing. There are both advantages and disadvantages to different stages.

The application of underglaze on bone-dry greenware is more fluid than on bisqueware because of the moisture content, but it is more difficult to do because the piece will still be in a fragile, unfired state. Bone-dry greenware can also get too damp, and moisture levels have to be controlled. If you make a mistake on greenware with underglazes, you'll have to scrape it off using a tool called a *rib* (a curved tool made of wood, metal, or plastic used for shaping, scraping, or smoothing clay objects).

If applying underglazes to bone-dry greenware before firing the piece for the first time, you should always bisque fire the piece afterwards, prior to applying the clear glaze coat.

If you choose to work on bone-dry ware before firing, you'll be able to make corrections or additions on top of the layer that you've already created after firing the piece to bisque. This approach gives you a second chance at the design, and an opportunity to layer designs and colors.

If your clay body isn't white, and you want bright colors, you should begin with clay that is in the leather-hard stage and apply a base coat of white slip to the clay. After the slip dries, you'll have a smooth surface on which to apply underglazes like paint on a white canvas.

Applying a commercially prepared underglaze with a calligraphy brush

Most beginners prefer to work on bisqueware because it is much easier to handle. You can remove mistakes by simply washing them off of the bisqued surface, which isn't possible when using underglazes on greenware. After washing, the bisqueware must dry for several hours—because the pores will be filled with water—before you will be able to work on it again.

Commercial underglazes are usually fired at low temperatures since some can burn out at higher temperatures. (The label of the product you choose will suggest the most suitable firing ranges for it.) A layer of clear glaze fired on top will enhance underglazes by making them appear brighter and glossier. Most underglazes, unlike glaze colors, bear almost the same color value before and after firing if fired at their optimum temperature.

Keep the following things in mind when applying underglazes:

■ A white plastic palette with cups comes in handy to pour out small amounts of the colors you are using. (You can also improvise with a foam egg carton.)

■ If underglazes are thinned down slightly with water, they will be translucent. Use them as if they are watercolors. They will absorb almost instantly into the piece.

■ Used straight from the tube or jar, underglazes will have more of an opaque effect.

■ Some potters prefer to work from light to dark with colors. In other words, painting dark colors over light may be more effective since some light underglaze colors will not show up if painted on darker ones.

My mother makes wonderful bran muffins. They are light and fluffy and delicious. She gave me the recipe so that I could make them. Even though I followed the same recipe and used the same ingredients, my muffins were more like doorknobs than anything resembling food.

So what's the difference? Anyone who cooks will agree that it is not only the recipe that makes the dish excellent, but the "touch" that you use in making it.

With cooking, touch is how you handle the ingredients. For applying surface decorations, it is:

— how you stir the slip
— how you hold the brush
— how you handle the pot
— how you apply the glaze
— how you load the kiln, the shelves
— how you fire the kiln…

Your personal touch is what ultimately makes the most difference in your work.

GLAZES

Have you ever walked along the beach and collected glistening colored stones and shells from the water's edge and put them in your pocket? Later, when you dug out your treasures, you couldn't figure out their original allure because their color had dried into an opaque dullness. The same holds true when comparing unglazed and glazed surfaces. Clear glazes serve as a vehicle for "wetting down" the surface of your piece. The glassy coating is reflective like water, causing underglaze colors to appear more vibrant and intense than they were before. Protecting the surface with a clear glaze will create a glossy surface that is light-reflective, durable, and food-safe if the piece is fired to vitrification. Glazes leave the clay body smooth, non-porous, and sometimes colored and textured.

In general, a glaze creates a glassy coating that is fused onto the surface of the clay after a ceramic piece is fired in the kiln. Glazes, like glass, are composed primarily of silica. But there is a lot more to glazes than just silica. The formulation of glazes is a science. Ingredients must be proportioned so that the glaze will adhere to the surface of the clay after melting. All glazes, whether they're matt or shiny, textured or glossy, colored or clear, include three essential components: *silica* (glass), also called flint, which melts at around 3100°F (1705°C); *fluxes*, which are compounds that combine with silica to make it melt at a lower temperature; and *alumina*, a refractory element that makes the glaze stronger and harder and prevents excessive running. Additional ingredients, including coloring oxides and stains, opacifiers, and fluxes suited to different firing temperatures, yield different glazing effects. Choosing a glaze requires a knowledge of which glazes will give you the desired surface, color, or texture that you want.

Tools for glaze preparation, application, and firing. (Clockwise from left: triple beam balance scale, 30-mesh screen, eye protection, kiln gloves, banding wheel, air compressor, wire wisk, surgical gloves, mortar and pestle, metal scoops, rubber spatula, respirator, and plastic containers)

Transparent Glaze Recipe/cone 04

The following is a widely used recipe for clear glaze.

Frit# 3195	88 g
Edgar's Plastic Kaolin	10 g
Bentonite	2 g

This formula adds up to 100 grams. I recommend making a 2000 gram batch for general purposes which makes about a gallon (3.84 L) of glaze. Multiply the recipe by 20 to get proper amounts.

Frit# 3195	1760 g
Edgar's Plastic Kaolin	200 g
Bentonite	40 g

Measuring mixed dry ingredients for making a glaze using a triple beam scale and bucket

Measure, weigh, and mix the dry ingredients. Pour approximately one gallon (3.84 L) of water into a bucket. Stir and dissolve the dry mixture.

Place a 30-mesh screen over another clean bucket and pour this mixture back and forth through the sieve at least twice. This will break up any lumps and give the glaze a smooth consistency like cream. After completing this process, the glaze is ready to use. Store it in a tightly sealed plastic container so that it doesn't evaporate. You can add water to the glaze if it does dry out.

Adding dry glaze ingredients to water in a bucket before mixing and sieving

Coloring a Transparent Glaze

To color a glaze, add .5-7% oxides (follow the chart in Appendix IX) or 5-15% stain to a batch. Weigh colorants out and add them to the other dry ingredients when using the recipe above or other glaze recipes. Stir until lumps are dissolved and the glaze is the consistency of milk. Thin with water if needed. Sieve to a clean bucket. Label the bucket with the name of the glaze.

Mixing dry glaze ingredients in water to dissolve them

Glazing Bisqueware

Remember that you usually do not glaze a piece until it has been bisque fired. (This

A test tile which shows the effect of a clear glaze and a colored clear glaze after firing on a bisque tile

means that if you've painted on a slip or underglaze, it should first be fired before applying a glaze to it.)

Choosing the right glaze for the work that you are doing is important. Commercially produced glazes have information on the label such as the temperature range at which they should be fired, color, recommended application method, ingredients, and whether or not they are foodsafe.

Steps to take in preparation for glazing:

1. Rinse or sponge off any dust or dirt from the piece in preparation for glazing it. After it has dried, shake out any shards or shavings that my have dropped inside the piece because they will contaminate your glaze if they end up getting poured into it during the process of glazing.

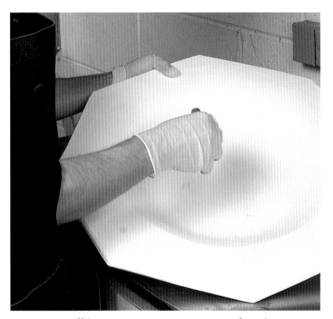

Sponging off bisqueware in preparation for glazing

2. If you have done sgraffito on your piece (see the last section of this chapter for a description of this technique), use a scrub brush and scrub your piece under the faucet for a few minutes to get rid of all of the burrs or rough edges that may be left around the lines that you have drawn. (When these are glazed they can be razor sharp.) If the burrs are stubborn, you may need to use sandpaper to get rid of rough edges. Let the piece dry overnight since it won't absorb glaze until it is dry again.

3. Place newspapers over the tables and floor area to save time cleaning.

4. Stir the glaze until well mixed. Sieve the glaze again if it seems at all lumpy. I recommend sieving the glaze before every use so that you can be assured your glaze is free from lumps and any contamination from shards.

5. After your piece has dried, use a bucket of clean water and a sponge to wipe off the bottom, or foot, of the piece. This is always done after glazing because if you have glaze on the foot it will melt and attach to the kiln shelf during firing.

Pouring the Glaze Inside a Piece

This is a convenient way to glaze the inside of a piece such as a bowl, cup, or other concave vessel.

Scoop or ladle the glaze to fill the interior of the vessel to the half way mark. Next, pour the glaze out immediately. (Don't let the glaze sit or it will become too thick on the surface because bisqueware is extremely absorbent.) After pouring the glaze out, sponge the rim to remove any drips.

Quickly pouring the glaze out of the coated piece into a wide-mouthed pan

Glazing the Exterior of a Piece

The following methods of brushing, pouring, and airbrushing may be used for glazing the exterior of a piece. I recommend that less-experienced potters brush on the clear glaze rather than pour it when coating the exterior or any convex surface of a piece. This method will give you the most control over the amount of glaze that you are applying. If you choose to pour the glaze on the exterior rather than brush it on, you should pay attention to the following suggestions. For assurance that you'll get an even coat of glaze, invest in a spraygun and compressor.

Ladling glaze into a charger

Brushing Dip the brush in glaze and saturate it, apply a stroke, allow it to absorb, and repeat until your surface is covered with an even coat of glaze. After doing this, there should be only a faint halo or outline of any underglaze decoration that you may have applied previously. If you can see your underglaze decoration too clearly, the glaze is too thin. If that is the case, simply apply another coat of glaze.

Pouring Find a way to hold your piece upside down (by the foot, if there is one) so that it can be held over the bucket of glaze. Using a cup or ladle, dip the glaze and coat the piece with it, allowing it to drip into a pan. Pour the glaze as quickly and evenly as possible, covering the entire piece in one movement. Try not to overlap the glaze too much since it may cause it to run in the firing or make clear glaze appear opaque. After coating the piece, wipe the glaze off the foot of the piece with a wet sponge after it has dried so that it won't stick to the kiln shelf during firing, unless you are planning to place it on pointed stilts. (Pointed stilts are heat-resistant supports used to raise glazed ware above the kiln shelf so that melted glaze won't fuse the ware to the shelf.)

Brushing the glaze onto a piece decorated with underglaze colors

The glaze after it has been brushed and has dried, covering all but a faint outline of the painted decoration

Using a container to pour the glaze onto the exterior of the charger, allowing the excess to run into a pan

Spraying After filling the container that attaches to the spraying mechanism, spray a test spot on newspaper to see if the glaze is thin enough. The glaze shouldn't hesitate when being sprayed, or drip, if it is the right consistency. If not, you can thin it slightly with water before spraying the whole piece.

Using a spray booth in a well-ventilated indoor or outdoor space, begin spraying evenly over the piece placed on a banding wheel. Don't pause in one area as you're spraying, or the area will get too saturated— keep moving. Coat the entire piece once; then repeat until you can see only a dim outline of your decoration. If it doesn't dry instantly you may be spraying too heavily or turning the banding wheel too slowly.

Lifting the piece off of the wheel with a bat placed on it in prepartion for turning it over and putting it back on the wheel

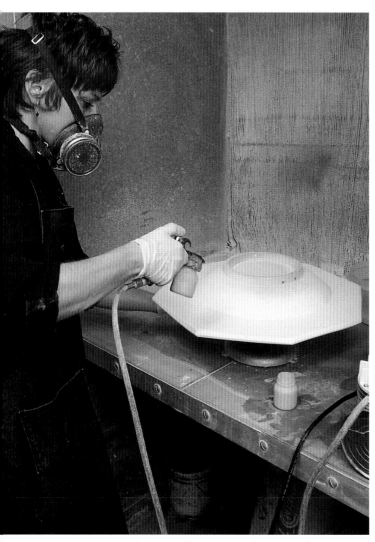

Spraying the bottom of a piece with glaze after placing it on a banding wheel in a spray booth

Placing the piece right-side up onto the wheel

Spraying the top of the piece with glaze

Crazing

Crazing, an unintentional effect that happens after firing the glaze, looks like a spider's web of cracks on the surface. It is caused when the glaze expands and contracts more than the clay body to which it is applied. In other words, the glaze does not properly "fit" the clay.

Crazing may be present when the ware is first taken from the kiln, or it may appear hours, days, or even years later. It may allow moisture to seep into the clay and cause it to be unhygienic.

Crazing is considered to be a glaze flaw, but it is difficult to avoid slight crazing. When you start examining industrial wares, you'll be surprised at the amount of crazing you'll find. A great deal of handmade pottery will have some form of it. You can work at eliminating it as you gain experience with glaze application and formulation.

Several factors can cause crazing: too heavy an application of glaze, underfiring the ware in a kiln that is not hot enough to fully melt the glaze, cooling the kiln too quickly, or removing the ware from the kiln in a hurry.

MAIOLICA

Maiolica has the most romantic heritage of all earthenware techniques. The story of maiolica begins in the thirteenth century when brilliantly colored and lustered wares known as "Majolica" from the island of Majorca off the coast of Spain were traded to the Italians. After artisans learned this technique from the Spanish, pottery industries sprang up across Italy to produce this glazed ware that was both beautiful and practical. It was particularly popular for use as pharmacy jars that contained herbs, oils, and medicines. In the creative fervor of the Renaissance, maiolica reached a new aesthetic level.

Maiolica is associated with Italy for both its technique and style, but other forms of tin-glazed earthenwares were produced in other countries. Similar polychrome wares were known as faience by the French, and the British referred to decorated tin-glazed Dutch ware as delft. There is also a tradition of tin-glazed earthenware in Portugal and middle eastern countries.

All of these names identify an "in-glaze" technique of ceramic decoration. An opaque, matt glaze is used to coat the unfired piece before oxides and stains are painted on top of this glaze. Both layers are then fired together, consequently melting and fusing the colors into the maiolica glaze. After firing, the colors become much brighter and darker.

Traditionally, maiolica glazes contained tin oxide as an *opacifier* (a material that causes a glaze to become opaque by producing minute crystals). Today, tin is not used as frequently because of expense. (For our purposes, we'll be using other ingredients for opacification.)

Maiolica differs from what are known as "overglaze" treatments because it is an in-the-glaze coloring process. *Overglaze* treatments are applied onto an already-fired glazed surface, which is then fired again at an even lower temperature. The next section will deal with this subject.

The following recipe for maiolica glaze is a popular, tried and true one that I recommend:

Matthias' Maiolica/cone 06-03

Frit 3124	83.34 g
Old Mine #4/Kentucky Ball clay	8.33 g
Edgar's Plastic Kaolin	8.33 g
Plus zircopax (opacifier)	11.11 g

Notice that, when added together, the first three lines of this formula add up to 100 grams. The opacifier is additional.

I recommend making a 5000-gram batch for general purposes—which makes about 2 ½ gallons (9.6 L) of glaze. Remember the rule of thumb to multiply the batch recipe by 10 for each 1000 grams that you want to increase it, as shown below:

Frit 3124	83.34 x 50 = 4167 g
Old Mine #4/ Kentucky Ball clay	8.33 x 50 = 416.5 g
Edgar's Plastic Kaolin	8.33 x 50 = 416.5 g
Plus zircopax (opacifier)	11.11 x 50 = 555.50 g

Steps for mixing:

1. Pour approximately 2 ½ gallons (9.6 L) of water into a bucket or fill half of a five-gallon (19.2 L) bucket. Add the dry ingredients, mix well, and allow them to dissolve over a few minutes.

2. Place an 80-mesh screen over another clean bucket and sieve the mixture twice (you'll have to sieve once into the clean bucket, then into the other bucket). Sieving the mixture twice will break up any lumps and smooth the glaze until it's the consistency of homogenized milk.

3. After sieving, add about ½ cup (120 mL or 85 g) of laundry starch to the mixture to add stiffness to the glaze. (Doing this will prevent the glaze from powdering and rubbing off when you apply colors later.) The starch should cause the glaze to be the consistency of cream.

4. Now you'll need to allow the glaze to stand overnight before you use it. The following day, you should sieve it again, and test it for proper consistency by dipping a tile or other sample piece in it. After it dries, the coverage should be smooth with no bubbles or pinholes.If you do have these problems, it means that the glaze is too thick and you should thin it down with water. A quick way to test for the right thickness is to scratch the surface of the piece with a pin tool or razor-sharp blade to see how thick the glaze is—it should be about 1/16 of an inch (1.6 mm) thick.

Mixing Maiolica Colors

The following section will tell you how to mix the colors that go on top of the maiolica glaze. I recommend using stains in the maiolica color mix below because they produce the truest colors. Every color imaginable is available to you, and colors can be layered in the painting stage for beautiful effects (we'll be demonstrating some of this in my projects later in the book). Stains also look almost the same when you paint them on as they will after the firing.

Mixing blue maiolica color

Maiolica Color Mix

This will be painted on top of the white maiolica glaze that we've just explored:

25 grams stain: 75 grams frit# 3124
or
1 part stain: 3 parts frit #3124

Use this combination for making black or dark blue because these colors need a higher proportion of frit:

25 grams stain: 100 grams frit# 3124
or
1 part stain: 4 parts frit #3124

Weigh out stains and frit and place in a 32-oz. (960 mL) or larger container (I use an empty yogurt container). Add water until the container is about two-thirds full and stir. For stirring maiolica color mixes, choose a stiff knife or other tool since the stain-frit solution hardens at the bottom of the container. (I have a collection of old kitchen butter knives that I use for mixing and remixing.) To keep color smudging to a minimum, add one tablespoon of laundry starch. Next add one teaspoon glycerine to make the brushing more fluid. Label the container and keep the lid on at all times unless in use.

Unfortunately, even after stirring, this color solution settles out almost instantly—so you'll have to stir it constantly when using it. If you use the color after it has settled out, your colors will be less intense since the depth of the color depends on the suspension of the mix and the amount of water in it. If there is too much water in the mix, the colors will appear diluted.

Bisque Firing in Preparation for Maiolica Glazing

I prefer to bisque fire a white slip coating onto the greenware, which provides a consistent and predictable surface on which to use the decoration, prior to beginning the maiolica process.

If you are using a white earthenware clay body, this is not necessary. However, I still prefer to do this step even when using such a body because slip will always make the surface smoother. The slip acts as a forgiving agent, covering any flaws. There will be less rough texture for the glaze to flow over and fewer pinholes.

To prepare bisqueware for maiolica glazing, rinse pieces off quickly so that they don't absorb too much water. Remove any shards that might be in the interior, then allow to dry several hours before glazing, or until the washed bisqueware is just slightly damp.

Glazing with Maiolica

I recommend the following techniques for applying maiolica glaze. Dipping and spraying work well, but I don't recommend brushing this type of glaze because every brush stroke will show and it's very difficult to get even coverage.

Dipping When glazing, stir the glaze constantly since it settles out quickly. Stirring well will help you to get a consistent coat of glaze on the piece. (Commercial additives may also be bought at ceramic suppliers which help to reduce glaze settling.)

To apply maiolica glaze, I recommend dipping. To do this, fill an appropriately sized container with enough glaze to submerge the entire piece. For larger pieces, you may have to use your imagination and use containers such as oil catchers or baby tubs.

You can create a foot ring on the body of your piece when constructing it to make glazing easier. Tongs, or any other tool for holding the piece, will work also, but afterwards you'll have to deal with spots that the glaze didn't touch where the tongs held the piece during glazing. You can touch the piece up with a paintbrush or sometimes smooth the glaze over with your finger when it is dry.

Spraying A sprayer and compressor also work well for applying maiolica glaze.

After filling the container that attaches to the spraying mechanism, try a test spot on newspaper to see if the glaze is the right consistency. If not, you can thin it slightly with water before spraying the whole piece.

Using a spray booth or a well-ventilated indoor or outdoor space, begin spraying the piece evenly. (Place the work on a banding wheel and keep it rotating to ensure even coverage.) Don't hesitate in one area as you're spraying, or it will get too saturated—keep moving. Coat the entire piece once—it should dry almost instantly. After the glaze dries, you should be able to scratch it with a pin tool and see about 1/16 of an inch (1.6 mm) of glazed thickness. Try to avoid drips. If the glaze does drip, you can later scrape off the glaze with a razor knife.

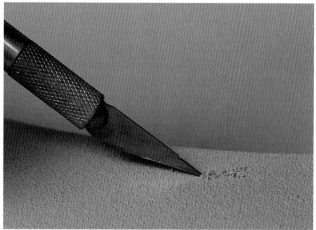

A razor knife can be used to remove glaze drips or to test glaze thickness.

Keep the following things in mind when applying maiolica:

■ Since maiolica is a matt glaze that will not flow or become liquid during the firing, any drip, drop, or overlap will show.

■ Too heavy an application may cause crawling, crazing, or pinholing of the glaze (see "flaws" section below).

■ Too thin an application will result in a surface that will probably not hold much of the maiolica color and may feel dry or rough to touch.

■ After glazing the piece, you should let the piece dry before sponging the bottom of it in order to do less damage to the surface of the glaze.

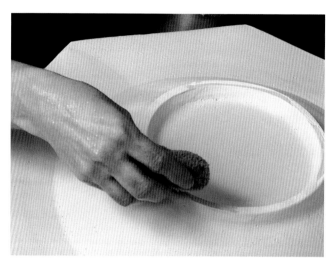

Sponging glaze off the bottom of a piece after drying to prevent it from sticking to kiln furniture

■ After the glaze has dried, if you have any pinholes (these look like tiny open pores, or pinpricks on the surface of the piece), rub them away with your finger.

Applying Maiolica Colors

To prepare for coloring maiolica pieces, allow them to dry at least twenty-four hours after glazing before decorating. If they are completely dry, the color will adhere much more easily.

The starch that you added to the glaze will help create a surface that won't chip, dust, or scrub off when you paint. Nevertheless, the sensitive surface created by the maiolica glaze will still need to be handled with care.

Before applying colors to your fresh white surface, do your homework by making thumbnail sketches and researching images that you want to include in your decoration. Then work out a detailed design in a sketchbook or on newsprint with a soft pencil.

When painting on the maiolica colors, handle the unfired glazed surface as little as possible. Continue to use a banding wheel for painting, just as you did with glazing. It is convenient to place the piece on a *bat* (a plaster, wood, or plastic disc) on top of the banding wheel while painting so that it can be transported easily later. If not wearing latex or rubber gloves while painting, you should wash your hands frequently since the stains contain chemicals. Washing will also help you to avoid transferring the stains around the piece.

Maiolica decoration in progress on a bisqued piece

Painting with Maiolica Colors

■ To apply the colors, use a soft-haired calligraphy brush (the kind that usually has a bamboo handle). These brushes will hold more color and don't scrub the surface. Stiff brushes tend to make the glaze dust off and chip, but can be useful for doing a dry-brush technique on the surface.

■ Experiment with different-sized brushes because each will make a distinct mark and leave a different amount of color. It is always best to try each brush out on a piece of paper prior to decorating your piece.

■ Like underglaze colors, maiolica colors will act very much like watercolors. Experiment with

them on a test piece to get the feel of the application before launching into a piece to be fired.

■ Begin with palest colors and work up to higher contrast colors. You can layer colors in this manner to create more depth. When layering some colors, a new color will be created. (You'll need to experiment with layering the colors on test pieces in order to learn what works best. Remember to record it in your test journal if you like the combinations that you find.)

■ If outlining images, do it as a last step with a dark color.

■ You can also create *sgraffito* lines (see techniques section at the end of this chapter for a description of sgraffito) on the surface after you've finished painting the piece. Try out various scribing tools such as a round-tipped ballpoint pen, a dull pencil, or the rounded handle-end of a small paintbrush for different line thicknesses and depth. The sgraffito mark will leave a white outline where the maiolica glaze shows through from underneath.

Glaze Firing Maiolica

Because maiolica is a low-fire technique, firing needs to take place in an electric kiln. (When fired in a gas reduction atmosphere, glaze flaws

A maiolica charger before and after glaze firing

are more frequent.) The glaze should dry at least 24 hours before loading the piece into the kiln to avoid steam evaporating from the surface and disrupting it during firing.

If you have a computerized kiln, program it to have a slow climb in temperature in the beginning of the firing and to down fire for a few hours after the completion of the firing.

Steps for glaze firing:

1. After placing the work in the kiln, switch the bottom electrical element on low for eight hours or overnight. This process of keeping the kiln at a constant temperature for a certain amount of time is called *heat soaking*. This process allows trapped gases to escape, and gives the glaze time to heal over after it bubbles up when melting. In other words, it will help to create a smoother surface. During this period, keep the kiln peep holes open and the lid propped open to allow gases to escape. Keep the kiln area well vented, unless you have an automatic venting system.

2. After heat soaking the work overnight, close the lid, wearing protective gloves. Put the kiln elements on low for four to six hours. Leave peep holes open.

3. Next, keep the peep holes open and put all elements on medium for four hours, or until they are bright red. Always wear protective eye wear such as goggles or glasses when looking into the kiln.

4. Now, seal up the peeps and turn all elements on high and fire for four to six hours, or until the cone melts. (Oftentimes an older kiln will fire more slowly.)

Possible Glaze Flaws After Firing

■ *Crazing*, found in most of the historical examples of maiolica, is a common flaw with this type of ware. It is usually caused by too heavy a glaze application, the pieces cooling too quickly, unloading the kiln when the temperature is above 500°F (260°C), or a bad fit between the glaze and clay body (if this is the case, then the easiest solution is to change the clay body).

■ *Crawling* occurs when the glaze separates from the clay in firing, leaving bare spots on the surface of the piece. It can be caused by too thick a glaze application, by dust or oil on the bisqued ware that keeps the glaze from absorbing properly, or by too rapid a warm-up in the glaze firing.

■ *White dots* are "freckles" that appear indiscriminately over the surface of the piece. These are caused by firing too fast, which doesn't allow the glaze time to release gases before cooling can take place. This can be corrected by regulating the rate of temperature change in the kiln.

MAIOLICA GALLERY

▶ **LINDA ARBUCKLE** (Micanopy, Florida), *Berry Bowl*, 10 x 2.5" (25 x 6.3 cm), 1997. Terra cotta. Maiolica. Δ03 firing.

▼ **TERRY SIEBERT** (Bainbridge Island, Washington), *Royal Teapot, Cup, and Saucer.* 11" height (27.5 cm), 1997. Terra cotta. Wheel thrown. Maiolica. Handpainted glazes. Δ04 firing. Photo by Wally Hampton.

◄ **MATT NOLEN** (New York, New York), *Sunshine Ewer*, 9" height (22.5 cm),1996. Handbuilt porcelain. Maiolica. Δ04 firing. Courtesy of Garth Clark Gallery, NYC.

▼ **POSEY BACOPOULOS** (New York, New York), *Covered Oval*, 5 x 12 x 4.5" (12.5 x 30 x 11.3 cm), 1998. Terra cotta. Wheel thrown, altered, and assembled. Slab base and lid. Pulled handles. Maiolica. Δ04 firing.

Photo courtesy of D. James Dee.

▲ **NAUSIKA RICHARDSON** (Dixon, New Mexico), *Pear Plate with Fish Border*, 11 x 11" (27.5 x 27.5 cm), 1997. Red earthenware. Slab plate made over hump mold. Maiolica glaze, stains and oxides. Sponged border. Δ06 bisque firing. Δ03 glaze firing. Photo by Pat Pollard.

▲ **JANET BELDEN** (Long Island City, New York), *Fish Vase*, 9 x 9 x 8.5" (22.5 x 22.5 x 21.3 cm), 1997. Red earthenware. Thrown and altered. Maiolica, brush and wax resist, glaze trailing, copper wash, stains. Δ04 firing. Photo by Algis Norvilla.

▶ **STANLEY MACE ANDERSEN** (Bakersville, California), *Tureen*, 10 x 12 x 12" (25 x 30 x 30 cm), 1997. Earthenware. Wheel thrown, handbuilt. Maiolica. Δ03 firing. Photo by Tom Mills.

▲ **Lisa Woollam** (Ontario, Canada), *Brier Island Mural*, 49.6 x
42.8 x 1.2" (124 x 107 x 3 cm), 1998. Red and white earthenware. Handbuilt and carved. Sprigs made from shells cast in plaster
to form press mold. Terra sigillata, oxides, maiolica, mason stains.
Sgraffito. Δ05 firing. Photo by artist.

▲ ▲ (top) **TERRY SIEBERT** (Bainbridge Island, Washington), *Sunflowers Bowl*, 16" diameter (40 cm), 1996. Terra cotta. Hump molded on wheel with thrown foot. Maiolica. Δ04 firing. Photo by Roger Schreiber.

▲ **W. MITCH YUNG** (Branson, Missouri), *Bowl*, 16 x 16 x 3" (40 x 40 x 7.5 cm), 1996. Red earthenware. Wheel thrown. Maiolica. Sgraffito. Δ04 firing. Photo by Jerry Anthony.

▲ ▲ (top) **LYNN PETERS** (Chicago, Illinois), *Home Sweet Home*, 18" diameter (45 cm), 1993. Pressed clay. Terra sigillata, slip, sgraffito. Δ04 firing. Photo by Jeff Martin.

▲ **MATTHIAS OSTERMANN** (Quebec, Canada), *Odysseus and the Sirens*, 18.4 x 4" (46 x 10 cm), 1997. White earthenware. Drape-molded slabbed clay over bisque mold with added thrown foot. Maiolica. Sgraffito. Δ05 firing. Photo by Jan Thijs.

OVERGLAZE ENAMELS/CHINA PAINTS

Overglaze enamels or *China paints* are colored surface decorations that are applied over a previously fired and glazed piece which is then fired again at low temperatures. For example, a piece can be decorated with an underglaze decoration such as slip, then glazed, and afterwards topped with overglaze decorations. By the end of this process, the piece will have been fired at least three times: first with underglaze decoration, then with a protective glaze, and last with overglazes. (Decals, discussed in the next section, are also applied over the glaze.)

Since these decorations are fired at a very low temperature, more layers of overglaze enamel can be added after the third firing and fired onto the surface. The process of refiring can be continued until you achieve the appearance that you want. The low-fire range of overglazes doesn't affect the clay body or the already intact glaze surface. In fact, it is normal to fire overglaze enamels several times, adding layers of color to build elaborate designs.

Mixing Overglaze Enamels

Overglaze enamels may be purchased premixed at ceramic supply stores. They come in small jars or tubes. Water-based enamels are easier to use and clean up than oil-based ones, since your brush can be washed out with water. Also, you won't be breathing the fumes associated with turpentine or mineral spirits which are used for cleaning with oil-based enamels.

You can also formulate your own enamels using dry-powdered ground colorants, stains, or commercially manufactured overglaze enamel powder and a wet medium made for this purpose. Again, I suggest using the water-based rather than oil-based medium. (It is possible to experiment with linseed oil and other non commercial products for mixing colorants, but I recommend starting with the commercial medium until you get a sense of the correct consistency for mixing.)

To mix your own enamels you'll need a mortar and pestle for grinding and a triple beam balance scale. The usual ratio for medium to colorant is two to one by weight. A ratio of medium to dry colorant is usually suggested on the jar or tube.

For a small batch, begin with 50 grams of colorant to 100 grams of medium. Weigh out the dry ingredients on the scale and put into the mortar. Measure the medium, add, and grind together with the pestle until fully mixed. The dry powder should be completely dissolved. To work well for brush painting, the mixture should be the consistency of yogurt.

Scrape the mixture out of the mortar with a rubber spatula and place it in an airtight container until ready for use. Repeat this process for each color that you want to use. The colors last only for one to two weeks, so mix them in small batches.

Painting with Overglaze Enamels

To prepare for painting with enamels, choose the colors and brushes that you want to use. I recommend the same type of soft-haired calligraphy brush as is used to paint maiolica colorants.

Above and next page: Applying finishing touches of overglaze enamels to a fired, slip decorated piece

Steps for applying overglaze enamels:

1. Place clean paper on your surface. Prepare your glazed piece for painting by wiping it with a damp cloth and drying it in order to create a dust-free surface on which to paint.

2. Use one coat of enamel. If the color is applied too thickly it will become dry in the firing. To thin the color while painting, simply add a little more medium if you're using studio-made enamels; commercially made enamels can be thinned with water if water-based, or mineral spirits if oil-based.

3. Enamels can also be airbrushed to create interesting effects. Thin them with the appropriate substance (water or solvent) until they are the consistency of milk. Keep the airbrush nozzle flushed out constantly in order to spray evenly.

4. Use a towel or sponge to wipe off mistakes. Remember that all marks, including smudges and fingerprints, as well as intentional strokes, will still be there after the piece is fired. A water-based medium is easier to clean off if you want to change something.

5. Allow the piece to dry for 8 to 24 hours. You can leave it on top of a cooling kiln or in the sun to dry it thoroughly before firing.

6. Fire the piece to cone 020-014 in a quick firing and cooling schedule, which will take five to eight hours depending on the kiln. You'll have to experiment with firing temperatures to see how your color comes out. If fired at too high a temperature or for too long, the colors will become dull or fire off. If you are firing too hot, drop down a cone or two in temperature. If your application burns off or fades, it might also mean that you need to use more color.

7. If the surface of your color looks dry instead of glossy after firing when using studio-made enamels, your application may contain too much colorant in relationship to the medium. If you are using paint from a jar or tube and this happens, your application was probably too heavy.

OVERGLAZE GALLERY

◄ **BERNADETTE STILLO**
(Philadelphia, Pennsylvania),
Hot/Cold, 5 x 10" (12.5 x 25 cm),
1997. Raku clay with kyanite.
Handbuilt around hand-formed
plaster shape, paddled. Impressed
with hand-carved clay stamps
and found textures. Copper matte
fumed glaze. Outside brushed with
copper/gold acrylic paint.
Δ01-1 firing. Photo by John Carlano.

▼ **JOAN TAKAYAMA-OGAWA**
(Pasadena, California), *Cherimoya
Tea Set*, 10 x 10 x 6" (25 x 25 x
15 cm),1996. Whiteware. Wheel
thrown. Underglazes, overglazes,
lusters. Multiple firings. Δ04 underglaze firing. Δ015-019 China
paint firing. Δ019 luster firing.
Courtesy of Ferrin Gallery, Northampton, MA.

▲ **CINDY KOLODZIEJSKI** (Venice,
California), *Dead Heat*, 11 x
6.75" (27.5 x 16.9 cm), 1991.
White earthenware. Luster.
Overglaze. Courtesy of Garth Clark
Gallery, NYC.

▲ **KURT WEISER** (Tempe,
Arizona), **Untitled**, 17 x 10"
(42.5 x 25 cm), 1992.
Porcelain clay. Overglaze
enamels. Courtesy of Garth Clark
Gallery, NYC.

◀ **JAMES KLUEG** (Duluth, Minnesota), *Culcha*, 19 x 10 x 4" (47.5 x 25 x 10 cm), 1997. Earthenware. Slab built. Stencil, overglaze brushwork, and sgraffito. Δ03 firing.

Photo by artist.

▶ **AMY KWONG** (Alberta, Canada), *Vase II*, 20 x 14 x 3" (50 x 35 x 7.5 cm), 1995. Earthenware. Slab pushed through plywood cut out to make vase shape. Edges scored and slipped then attached. Underglaze, commercial overglaze.

Photo by artist.

▲ **ROBIN C. MANGUM**
(Sparta, North Carolina), ***Short and Stout***, 18 x 16 x 12" (45 x 40 x 30 cm), 1998. White earthenware. Wheel thrown (altered), hand sculpted. Satin overglaze. Δ03 bisque firing. Δ04 glaze firing. Photo by Tim Barnwell.

▲ **MICHAEL CARLIN** (Burgettstown, Pennsylvania), ***Somnambulist***, 28 x 9 x 9" (70 x 22.5 x 22.5 cm), 1992. White earthenware. Handbuilt on armature. Underglaze, China paint, platinum luster. Δ04 firing. Δ018 firing for luster. Photo by artist.

DECALS

Decals are an increasingly popular mode of applying images to the surface of ceramics. In this process, an image or a design printed with a screen on special paper is usually transferred to a glazed surface and fired on. The image then becomes a permanent part of the piece. This technique makes well-rendered images available to you without having to create complex drawings.

In the following section, we'll describe how to make and apply your own decals to your ware using overglaze enamels and a printing screen. Then we'll discuss applying them to a glazed piece of work. An example of this process is illustrated in Chapter Three, so flip ahead while reading if you want to see photographs of it being done.

Creating and Using Decals

Learning to make and apply decals will allow you to use several images on the same piece or create collage effects if you choose. Decals are also effective on top of glazed surfaces that have been decorated with underglaze painting. Overglaze painting is often used in conjunction with decals to highlight areas of the printed image with color and line.

The possibilities are endless. But, first, you must master the printing technique, which takes time. With practice, you'll find it to be a fascinating way to enhance the surfaces of your pieces.

Making a Screen

The first step to making a decal is creating a screen from your image. This screen will be

Clockwise from upper left: Studio-made decals, tubes and semi-moist pans of overglaze enamels, decal paper, squeegee, containers of powdered enamel colors, screens

used to make a print which will eventually be transferred to the glazed surface of your piece.

You can use clip art, photographs, drawings, computer-generated images, prints, collages, or any black-and-white image that is camera-ready and sized to fit on your piece. (Photocopying an image and reducing or enlarging it will work if you need to change the size. If using images that have been printed in books or magazines, be aware of rules of copyright.)

If you have access to a darkroom, you can learn to produce your own screen image. However, this process is time-consuming and complicated. Since most potters are not also photographers, images are usually sent to a professional print shop for the creation of a screen. This process can usually be completed in three to five days.

To locate a company, check your local yellow pages and find a full-service printer. If your artwork can be put on a computer disk, it's even more convenient for the printer.

Remember that your original image must be the exact size that you want to print. Ask for a screen mesh size of at least 75, but no larger than 150. If your image is very detailed, opt for the larger number of threads. The screen of your image will come back to you in a frame (either wood, metal, rubber, or plastic) which will stabilize the mesh so that it can be used for printing.

Printing

In order to print, you will need to purchase decal paper—a special paper made to work with ceramic medium. You can buy this at a ceramic supply house. It is not possible to substitute anything else for this paper.

The edge of the decal paper should be cut about an inch (2.54 cm) larger than the image on the screen in preparation for applying the image.

Materials for Printing

- newspapers to place on table while working

- overglaze enamel colors/China painting powders

- mixing medium for colorants

- a mortar and pestle to grind colorant and medium

- a rubber spatula with which to manipulate the colorant

- a squeegee for printing

- plain paper for practice printing of your image

- a sponge to clean the screen

- a fan to dry the screen quickly

- polyurethane

- a soft brush to apply polyurethane

- prints

- a pair of scissors with which to clip images

- airtight zippered plastic bags in which to store finished prints

Set-up in preparation for printing decals: mixed overglaze enamels, squeegee, decal paper, screens

Steps for printing:

1. Set up your work space near a sink. Choose a dark color for printing that will make your image show up well. For this application, you'll be using only one color of ink since creating different screens and registrations for more than one color is complicated for a beginner.

2. Mix the medium and overglaze enamel/China paint colorants following the directions on the packaging. (Dry sieve the overglaze enamel dry powder through a 30-mesh screen before wet mixing to assure that you are using the finest particles for mixing. Taking the time to do this will simplify the mixing process.) The usual mix is approximately a two to one ratio of medium to powder. You could use a premixed enamel for this purpose, but it will be more expensive and you won't be mixing the exact amount that you need.

3. Begin by mixing together 200 grams of medium and 100 grams of powder. The mixture will have a cottage cheese texture. Keep mixing it until the powder is totally dissolved and blended. The mixture should remain quite thick, much thicker than inks that you might use for non-ceramic silk screening.

4. Cover your work table with newspaper. Align and register the screen over the decal paper ready to receive the ink. (If someone can help hold the screen to assist you with this process, it's easier.)

5. Use the rubber spatula to spread approximately 1/2-inch (1.27 cm or 13 mm) coverage of ink over the screen's image. Do this gently, as if you were icing a cake, so that the ink will rest on top of the screen and not penetrate it.

6. Properly register the screen on the practice paper, holding it above the paper, lining up the edges of the screen with the paper so that there is plenty of room to print the image. Using both hands, and starting at the top of the screen, tilt the squeegee slightly up with the rubber edge placed firmly on the screen in preparation for the descent down the screen. With an even and firm movement, drag the squeegee over the surface of the screen, pressing the ink through it so that it prints onto the paper underneath. You'll need to work quickly with the ink when it is on the screen because it dries rapidly. Practice this process several times to get a feel for it. Make sure you are comfortable with the process before attempting it on the actual decal paper.

7. The screen will probably need to be washed after every three to five prints. After scraping off the leftover ink with the spatula, rinse to dry for at least eight hours.

8. When the prints are dry, paint a thin coat of polyurethane over them with a soft brush. Allow them to dry for eight hours.

9. When these are dry, layer them between plain paper, and store them in an airtight zippered plastic bag until you're ready to use them.

Steps for applying decals:

1. Remember that ceramic decals need to be applied to a glaze-fired piece because they need a smooth surface in order to adhere. Any glazed surface will work, including one onto which you've already painted and fired underglaze decoration, painted overglaze enamels, or fired with a clear or white glaze. Wipe the piece clean with a damp cloth to ensure it is free of dust and grease before applying decals.

2. You should plan your design beforehand, and then cut the decals to the size and shape that you want.

3. Soak them in a bowl of clean water for about five minutes until the paper curls. They are ready to use when the image appears to loosen from the paper.

4. Remove them from the water and gently coax the printed image off the paper and hold it in the air by its corners. Be careful not to tear it. It will have the fragile texture of a butterfly's wing. With the decal still suspended, begin laying the free end onto the surface of the piece. Press the decal on slowly as you lower it onto the surface, removing any air

Pressing a decal onto the surface of a piece

bubbles and excess water as you go along with your fingers or a sponge. Next, blot off any remaining water from the surface.

5. Apply all the decals in this manner and check afterwards to make certain that there are no trapped air bubbles or pockets of water. If there are bubbles, use a razor or matt knife to prick the surface and gently rub them out with your finger until gone. You can also press from the center of the decal out to the edge with your fingers to eliminate bubbles.

6. Pat the surface dry and apply overglaze enamels from tubes or jars if you desire.

7. The decals and painting need to dry for at least eight hours. You can allow them to sit in the sun or on top of a warm kiln.

8. Fire to between cone 020-014.

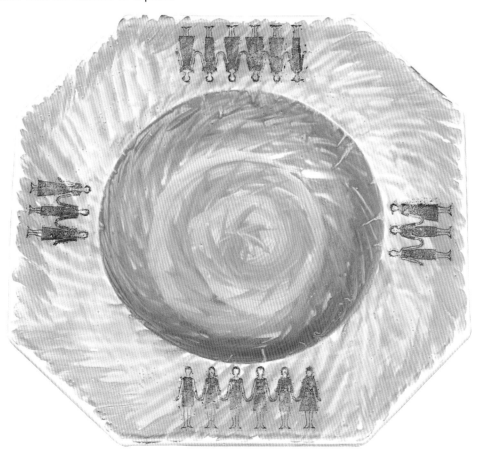

The finished piece after firing

DECAL GALLERY

◀ **SARAH E. WILLIAMS** (Jamaica Plain, Massachusetts), *Feminine Protection*, 7 x 9 x 4.5" (17.5 x 22.5 x 11.3 cm), 1998. White earthenware. Handbuilt, slipcast. Decals and flocking. Clear glaze. Δ04 bisque firing. Δ04 glaze firing. Δ020 decal firing. Photo by Dean Powell.

▼ **MARK BURLESON** (Asheville, North Carolina), *Excellent, Everlasting*, 92 x 30" (230 x 75 cm), 1998. Terra cotta. Slab construction. Textural glazes, photo decals, luster, underglaze, overglaze, ceramic watercolor, photo transfer, China paint. Δ06-04 firing. Δ018-016 firing for luster, decals, overglazes. Photo by N. Pickett.

▲ **VICTOR SPINSKI** (Newark, Delaware), *Ash Tray*, 10 x 10 x 4" (25 x 25 x 10 cm), 1997. Handbuilt, slip cast, carved, extruded. Photo decals, lusters. Δ04 firing. Photo by Bobby Hansson.

▶ **VERNE FUNK** (San Antonio, Texas), *Texas Mona*, 12 x 12 x 1.5" (30 x 30 x 28.8 cm), 1996. Whiteware. Slip, under-glaze pencil, decal, luster, matte and gloss glaze. Δ04 bisque firing. Δ06 glaze firing. Δ018 decal and luster firing.

LUSTERS

I am often asked about lusters, which are a type of metallic coating that is applied to a glazed surface or clay body and fired to a low temperature, creating an iridescent sheen. While they are beautiful and desirable, I avoid using in the school environment. The jury is still out about lusters, because, like so many aspects of our lives in this modern world, there are undefined health risks involved with using them.

Many contemporary ceramicists use lusters in a controlled environment. With experience, they can be effectively used to create seductive results, as you can see from the examples in this book. If you decide to use them, be sure that you understand thoroughly the health risks that are involved.

LUSTERS GALLERY

◄ **CAROL GOUTHRO** (Seattle, Washington), *Oakleaf Vase*, 22 x 17 x 11" (55 x 42.5 x 27.5 cm), 1998. Terra cotta. Wheel thrown, handbuilt, and slip cast sections assembled at leather-hard stage. Leaves, branches carved at leather-hard stage. Faux wood carved through underglazes at bone-dry stage. Underglazes, glazes, lusters. Δ04 bisque firing. Δ05 glaze firing. Δ019 luster firing. Photo by Roger Schreiber.

▶ **JOAN TAKAYAMA-OGAWA** (Pasadena, California), *Chalices*, 10 x 4 x 4" (25 x 10 x 10 cm), 1998. Whiteware. Molded, slip cast, extruded, wheel thrown. Sgraffito. Underglazes, glazes, overglazes, lusters. Multiple firings of 6-8 times. Δ08 bisque firing. Δ04 underglaze firing. Δ015-019 China paint firing. Δ019 luster firing. Photo by Steven Ogawa.

▶ **MARCIA JESTAEDT** (Bowie, Maryland), *Lavender in My Garden*, 48 x 40 x .75" (120 x 100 x 2 cm), 1997. Raku clay. Chipped background. Sgraffito. Commercial glazes, lusters, gold paint. Δ04-06 glaze firing. Photo by Breger and Associates.

▲ **Carol Gouthro** (Seattle, Washington), **Teapot**, 8 x 12 x 8" (20 x 30 x 20 cm), 1998. Terra cotta. Slip cast body, hand-built spout and handle. Underglazes, glazes, lusters. Δ04 bisque firing. Δ05 glaze firing. Δ019 luster firing.
Photo by Roger Screiber.

◄ **Joan Takayama-Ogawa** (Pasadena, California), **Mad Hatter's Tea Party,** 14 x 15 x 12" (35 x 37.5 x 30 cm), 1998. Whiteware. Wheel thrown, slab construction. Underglazes, glazes, over-glazes, lusters. Δ08 bisque firing. Δ04 underglaze firing. Δ015-019 China paint firing. Δ019 luster firing. Photo by Steven Ogawa.

◄ **Marylou Higgins**
(Pittsboro, North Carolina), **Green Apple Tea Time**, 14.5 x 10 x 7" (36.3 x 25 x 17.5 cm), 1997. Stoneware. Formed and trimmed clay. Slip, underglaze paint and pencils, glaze, luster. Δ07 bisque firing. Δ07 glaze firing. Δ018 luster firing. Photo by Edward Higgins.

▲ **Lisa Maher** (La Jolla, California), **Slippers**, 3 x 3 x 7" (7.5 x 7.5 x 17.5 cm), 1996. Stoneware. Luster. Δ06 firing.

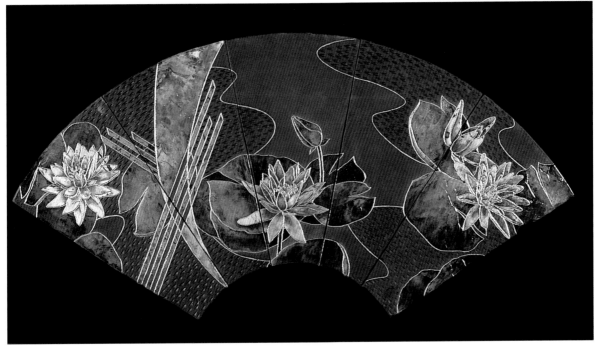

▲ **Marcia Jestaedt** (Bowie, Maryland), **Evening Blossoms**, 17.5 x 35.5 x .75" (44 x 89 x 2 cm), 1997. Raku clay. Chipped background. Sgraffito. Commercial glazes, lusters, gold paint. Δ04-06 glaze firing. Photo by Breger and Associates.

TECHNIQUES

The following are application methods most commonly used for decorating with slips and underglazes. Brushing, sponging, stencilling, and fake airbrushing may also be used with maiolica and overglaze enamels. Chapter 3 shows demonstrations of all of these techniques, and as you read, you may want to refer to that chapter to get a first-hand look at the process.

An assortment of tools to use for decorating ceramic pieces

Brushing

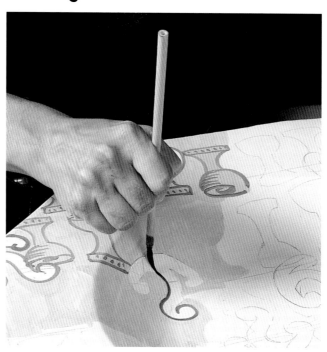

Applying an outline to a maiolica decoration with a calligraphy brush

Because so much of surface decoration is painting, brushwork is the foundation of all decorated ceramics. Learning to use a brush and paint is something that is both exhilarating and frustrating at times. Entire books have been written on the subject, including those on technique as well as design.

Nevertheless, the best way to learn to paint is to gather a few ideas and begin. Test your brush strokes on a sketch pad or other paper suited for painting. Remember that painting on bisqueware is much like watercolor or tempera painting—the paint absorbs quickly into the surface. Because of this, you have to work from light to dark with colors. Enamels, used on top of a glazed surface, are thicker and more akin to acrylics or oils.

Brushes come in all shapes and sizes, and degrees of stiffness or pliability. They also have a wide range of cost depending upon whether they are made of natural or synthetic hair.

I use a soft Chinese calligraphy brush for a lot of my decoration. However, any brush that creates the effect that you want shouldn't be passed up. Investigate by looking at brushes in ceramic supply houses, art supply stores, and even hardware stores. Pick them up and pluck them to feel how soft or hard they are. And, as always, experiment and find the ones that are the most comfortable for you to use. Choosing brushes, like choosing surface decorations, can be a very personal thing.

Sponging

Sponging slip on top of a cutout

Sponging on slips, underglazes, or enamels with a synthetic or natural sponge creates a stippled effect on the surface. Different sponges naturally create varying textures, and sponges can be used to layer contrasting colors. Sponging a very dark color over a bright color on your surface can create a dramatic effect. You can also create gradations of color by sponging from a light color to a dark one.

Stencilling/Paper Cutouts

Removing a "negative" paper cutout

Stencilling uses paper cutouts (blotting paper, or other paper that is not glossy, works well) to create a positive or negative image of a design. To make a positive image, simply cut one from paper, soak in water, and then press it onto the surface with a damp sponge. It will adhere while you paint, sponge, or airbrush color on top of it.

Both parts of the stencil can be used to make an image: the one that you cut out in the shape that you want (the positive image) or the part that you've cut away (the negative image). To use a negative image, use the part of the paper that you cut away, wet it down and apply it, then fill in color.

Paper stencil cutouts are great fun with which to experiment, and you can alter them as you go along with your design, repeating but changing an image on a piece. They are great for layering color as well as design.

Sgraffito

Using a tool to make sgraffito lines

Sgraffito is an old ceramic drawing technique which began with the use of white slip over reddish clay which was then scratched to reveal the clay underneath. The same technique is used today with more choices—colored clays in the leather-hard or bone-dry stage can be covered with coatings of contrasting underglazes or colored slips and then scratched to reveal layers beneath the surface. For example, if you have a red earthenware body, and you have layered a white slip over it, you can draw through the white slip to the red clay underneath. If you are using a white clay body, you might use a darker contrasting slip, and draw through it to the clay underneath. You can also carefully scratch through a layer of color to reveal a layer of glaze beneath (this works well with maiolica since the maiolica glaze underneath the color is white). Sgraffito will add texture to your surface since you are actually carving down into the clay or slip. For this reason, it is usually done as a last technique on the surface.

After the surface color is dry, a sgraffito tool such as a pen nib, ball point pen, dull pencil, dental tool, or end of a small paintbrush is used to draw the lines on the surface. When using this technique, make note of how you have layered the slips in order to achieve different colors of line. There will be burrs or drag marks from the excess slip or underglaze that you remove. If they are heavy, you are working the slip when it is too wet. You should always wait until the slip is leather hard before using sgraffito. When the burrs are bone dry, they will come off neatly if swept with a soft brush.

Slip Trailing

Trailing the slip with a squeeze bottle

What is known as *slip trailing* was used as far back as the fifteenth century in Europe, when slips were squeezed into decorative motifs and then feathered at right angles using a comb or feather.

Slip trailing is a decorating technique that adds texture or bulk to the clay surface. Rather than carving down into the clay as with sgraffito, you draw a beaded line on the surface of the piece.

Slip trailing works best on clay in the early leather-hard stages, but some slips will work on bone-dry or bisqued ware. Since slip is made of clay, it is important to think about how it will fit the clay after it dries. If it doesn't fit, it will drop off. When successful, it creates a relief texture on the surface.

To trail slip, sieve the slip first to remove large particles and pour it into a bottle with a nozzle such as a ketchup bottle, hairdresser's squeeze bottle, or a cake decorating tube. Different widths of line may be achieved by the touch that you use with the application. Moving slowly will bring you a wider line, moving quickly will stretch the slip. Slip can be used in a precise manner to draw lines, but it is also a great improvisational technique. Feathering can be created with the slip by dragging a brush or feather through the beaded line.

Like sgraffito, slip trailing should be done as the last technique on the surface, since it is difficult to add anything further to your painting after creating a raised texture with the slip.

Fake Airbrushing

Using a toothbrush to spatter paint in a "fake airbrushing" technique

Before undertaking this technique, clear a surface on which to put your piece with paper underneath. Remove any other open containers of color or other work that might get an accidental coating. To try this fun technique, get an old toothbrush, load it up with slip or underglaze color, and pluck the color onto the surface of the piece using a front to back motion. The quickness of your movement, the amount of paint on the brush, and the angle and height from which you splatter the color will create different effects. You can use more than one color and mix them, grade the colors, or create a light to dark range. Try other brushes with this technique—experiment and invent something new!

▲ **SHERYL MURRAY-HANSEN**
(Portland, Oregon), *Standing in
Sunflowers*, 5.75 x 4.75 x 2.5"
(14.4 x 12 x 6.3 cm), 1997.
Low-fire commercial terra cotta
slip. Slip cast from carved slab.
Carved with low relief.
Commercial underglazes, clear
glaze. Δ04 bisque firing. Δ06
glaze firing. Photo by Phil Harris.

◄ **CARY ESSER** (Kansas City,
Missouri), *Campsis Radicans
Triptych*, Each section: 16 x
6.5 x 1" (40 x 16.3 x 2.5 cm),
1996. Red earthenware. Press-
molded tile (bas relief). Terra
sigillatas applied at unfired
stage followed by glaze at
bisqued stage. Δ04 firing.
Photo by Seth Tice-Lewis.

▲ **MICHEL LOUISE CONROY** (San Marcos, Texas), *Vase from the Still/Stir Series*, 23.5 x 9 x 9" (58.8 x 22.5 x 22.5 cm), 1992. White earthenware. Wheel thrown in stages with coil and throw method. Slips in layers. Glaze. Δ04 bisque firing. Δ06 glaze firing.
Photo by the artist.

▲ **KATHY TRIPLETT** (Weaverville, North Carolina), *Window Tea*, 22 x 11 x 10" (55 x 27.5 x 25 cm), 1998. White earthenware. Slab and extruded. Terra sigillata, glaze over black copper oxide wash. Δ05 firing.
Photo by Tim Barnwell.

◄ **PAUL SACARIDIZ** (Chicago, Illinois), **Untitled**, 5 x 5' (12.5 x 12.5 cm), 1996. Terra cotta and wood frame. Tiles hand-pressed in plaster mold. Stencilled letters. Wax applied around letters. Terra sigillata, textured crawl glaze. Δ04 firing. Photo by Jennifer Lapham.

► **ANTONIO FINK**
(Philadelphia, Pennsylvania),
Yellow (from The Four Seasons),
40 x 1.8 x 2" (1.10 m x 4.4 cm
x 5 cm), 1997. Raku clay. 160
hand-cut tiles using a wooden
stencil. Commercial underglazes
and glazes. Δ06 firing. Photo by
John Carlano.

▼ **VIRGINIA SCOTCHIE**
(Columbia, South Carolina),
Double Head, 36 x 19 x 13"
(90 x 47.5 x 32.5 cm), 1997.
Terra cotta. Coil and slab. Glaze
applied in thick coat to create
textured surface. Δ08 firing.
Photo by Peter Lenzo.

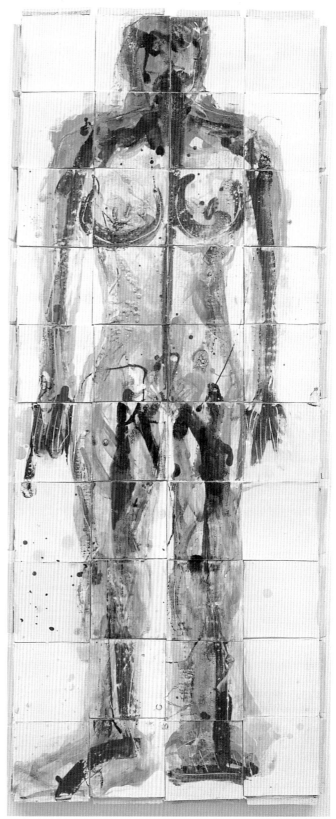

◄ **VERNE FUNK** (San Antonio, Texas), *No Smoking*, 31.5 x 29 x 9" (78.8 x 72.5 x 22.5 cm), 1996. Whiteware. Slab construction. Details cast in press mold. Slip. Luster. Sgraffito. Wood base. Δ04 bisque firing. Δ06 glaze firing. Δ018 luster firing. Photo by artist.

▼ **JOHN WERBELOW** (Gillette, Wyoming), *Chris' Dream*, 12 x 9" (30 x 22.5 cm), 1997. White earthenware. Wheel thrown, trimmed, sanded. Drawing with underglaze pencils, sealed with clear glaze. Photo by artist.

▲ **VICTOR SPINSKI** (Newark, Delaware), *Box with Tools*, 15 x 10 x 8" (37.5 x 25 x 20 cm), 1998. Low-fire clay. Cast, hand-built, slip cast, carved, sand-blasted. Lusters, glazes, stains. Δ04 bisque firing. Δ05-06 glaze firing. Δ018 luster firing.
Photo by Bobby Hansson.

▶ **MARC LEUTHOLD** (Potsdam, New York), *Yellow Disc*, 23 x 23 x 1" (57.5 x 57.5 x 2.5 cm), 1997. Earthenware. Carved at leather-hard stage. Terra sigillata applied at bone-dry stage. Δ04 low-fire salt vapor bisque firing.
Photo by Eva Heyd.

▲ **MICHAEL KIFER** (Richland, Michigan), *50/50 Platter*, 20 x 20 x 3" (50 x 50 x 7.5 cm), 1998. White earthenware. Slab over hump mold. Δ02 bisque firing. Δ05 glaze firing. Photo by artist.

▲ **IRMA STARR** (Kansas City, Missouri), *Alfred Commemorative Plate*, 12 x 8" (30 x 20 cm), 1998. Earthenware. Slip trailing emulating 17th century slipware techniques. Δ04 firing.

◀ **PATRICK DOUGHERTY** (Penland, North Carolina), *Jonah's Dream*, 4 x 24" (10 x 60 cm), 1998. White earthenware. Wheel-formed. Slip trailing. Underglazes. Clear glazes. Δ03 bisque firing. Δ05 glaze firing. Photo by Jonathan Wallen.

▶ **Lynn Peters** (Chicago, Illinois), *Floral Earth Charger*, 22" diameter (55 cm), 1995. Pressed earthenware clay. Terra sigillata, slip, sgraffito. Δ04 firing. Photo by Jeff Martin.

▼ **Matthias Ostermann** (Quebec, Canada), *Odysseus and the Sirens*, 18.4 x 4" (46 x 10 cm), 1997. Earthenware. Drape-molded slabbed clay over bisque mold with added thrown foot. Maiolica. Sgraffito. Δ05 firing. Photo by Jan Thijs.

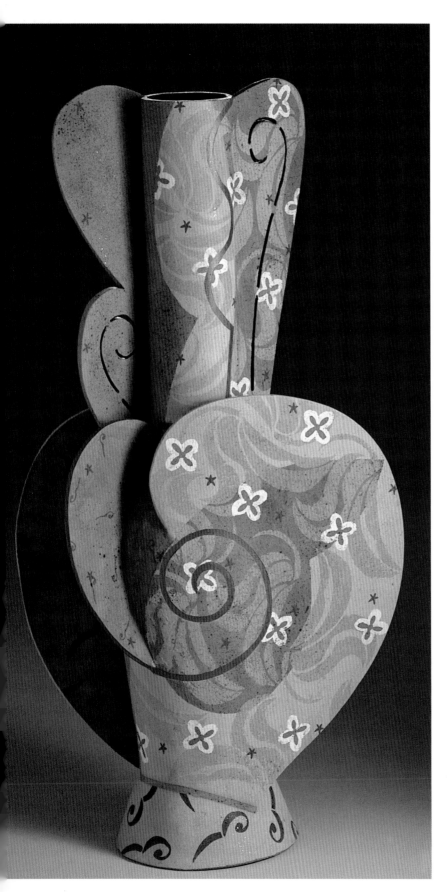

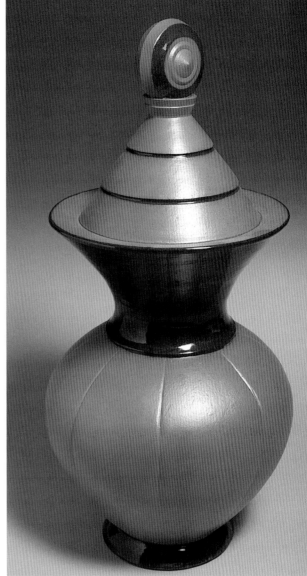

▲ **MARK JOHNSON** (South Portland, Maine), *Jar*, 20 x 10 x 10" (50 x 25 x 25 cm), 1997. Red earthenware. Thrown and assembled parts. Terra sigillata, slip, glaze. Δ04 firing. Photo by artist.

◄ **ANDREA GILL** (Alfred, New York), *Persian Ornament*, 47 x 25 x 12" (117.5 x 62.5 x 30 cm), 1996. Terra cotta. Slab built using press molds and handbuilding. Slips applied with stencils and brushes, clear glaze applied with toothbrush. Δ03-07 firing.

▲ **Sharon Fliegelman**
(Topanga, California), **Untitled**, 7 x 5.5 x 5.5" (17.5 x 13.75 x 13.75 cm), 1998. Casting slip. Underglazes. Monoprinted with silkscreen, brushing, spattering, stamping. Δ06 firing. Photo by artist.

▲ **Robin Campo** (Chamblee, Georgia), **Hot Potato**, 9 x 3 x 9" (22.5 x 7.5 x 22.5 cm), 1998. White earthenware. Slip cast and assembled. Terra sigillata, laquer, salt and copper sulfate. Copper wire. Δ010 bisque firing. Raku firing for 6 hours. Photo by artist.

▶ **Posey Bacopoulos** (New York, New York), **Beaked Pitcher**, 5 x 8 x 4" (12.5 x 20 x 10 cm), 1997. Terra cotta. Wheel thrown, altered, and assembled. Maiolica. Δ04 firing. Photo by D. James Dee.

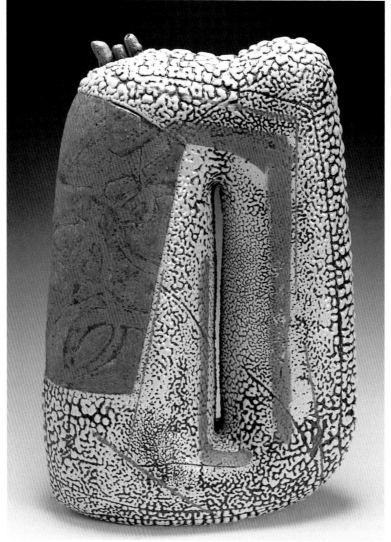

▲ **LINDA HUEY** (Alfred Station, New York), *Hidden Assortment*, 16 x 14 x 3" (40 x 35 x 7.5 cm), 1995. Terra cotta. Handbuilt. Colored glazes. Δ04 firing. Photo by artist.

◄ **YOSHIRO IKEDA** (Manhattan, Kansas), *Growth*, 22 x 12 x 6" (55 x 30 x 15 cm), 1998. Stoneware. Coiled. Sprayed. Wax resist. Δ02,03, and 06. Photo by Scott Dooley.

▲ **JANET BELDEN** (Long Island City, New York), *Fish Plate*, 12" diameter (30 cm) ,1996. Red earthenware. Wheel thrown. Maiolica, brush and wax resist, copper wash, glaze stains. Δ04 firing. Electric.
Photo by Algis Norvilla.

▶ **CAROL GOUTHRO** (Seattle, Washington), *Tulip Vase*, 22 x 16 x10" (55 x 40 x 25 cm), 1998. Terra cotta. Wheel thrown, handbuilt and slip cast sections assembled at leather-hard stage. Carved leaf forms. Flowers formed in wet clay and added. Underglazes, terra sigillata, clear and matt glazes, lusters. Δ04 bisque firing. Δ05 glaze firing. Δ019 luster firing.
Photo by Roger Schreiber.

◄ **DEBORAH BLACK** (Toronto, Canada), *Teapot*, 7.5 x 10.5 x 3.5" (18.8 x 26.3 x 8.8 cm), 1998. Red earthenware. Handbuilt with slabs. Slips, glazes. Δ04 firing.

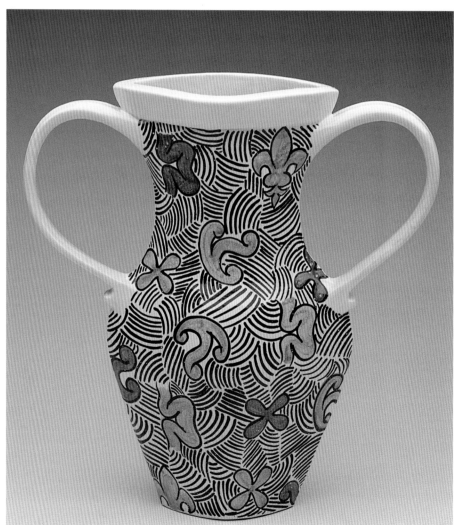

► **LYNN PETERS** (Chicago, Illinois), *Mixed Message*, 20" height (50 cm), 1997. Red earthenware. White slip under maiolica glaze. Δ04 firing.

Photo by Jeff Martin.

▲ **Lisa M. Naples** (Doyleston, Pennsylvania), *Cream and Sugar*, 5 x 4.5 x 3.5" (12.5 x 11.3 x 8.8 cm), 1997. Handbuilt with slabs. Slips, glazes. Δ04 firing.

▶ **Terry Siebert** (Bainbridge Island, Washington), *Meadow Pitcher*, 22" height (55 cm), 1995. Terra cotta. Wheel thrown. Incised white slip with clear and colored glazes. Δ04 firing. Photo by Roger Schreiber.

APPLICATION IN ACTION
Seeing It Done Firsthand

The lyfe so short, the crafte so long to lerne.

-Geoffrey Chaucer

On the following pages, I'll demonstrate the applications and techniques for low-fire surface decoration that you've read about so far. Refer to the sections on specific applications and techniques if you need more detail on certain subjects.

I used a charger form because it provides a wonderful surface to decorate. But visualize any of these techniques on another form with a smooth surface to decorate (be it a vase, bowl, or sculpture), and you'll be on your way. Use your imagination and change the colors of the applications, the shapes, and the techniques that are combined. Make the undertaking of low-fire surface decoration your own personal adventure. That's what I've always done!

FROG CHARGER
Slips, Cutouts, Sgraffito, and Slip Trailing

APPLICATIONS/MATERIALS

*Leather-hard earthenware
  charger*
Red terra sigillata
Chinese calligraphy brush
Paper cut out
White slip

Hakeme brush
Pencil
Matt knife
Plastic squeeze bottle
Black slip

1. If possible, always place the work you are decorating on a banding wheel. Here, I've put a leather-hard earthenware charger on a wheel and am applying the first coat of red terra sigillata. Using a Chinese calligraphy brush, I'm slowly turning the piece on the wheel while dragging the brush in a progressive spiral outwards toward the rim. This technique creates a nice even coat.

3. With cutout secured, I'm ready to apply the next coat of white slip. I'm applying it with a wider brush called a hakeme brush which creates a wide sweep with which to cover the cutout, again turning the wheel while applying and working toward the outside edge of the piece.

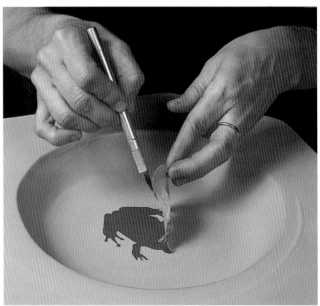

2. Now that the terra sig is dry, I'm applying, through gentle pressure, a cutout of a frog that has first been soaked in water so that it will adhere to the surface. I chose the center of the piece for the cutout so that I can create radiating designs around it later.

4. Now, after the slip has dried for several minutes, I've used a matt knife to find the cutout underneath the surface of the white terra sig. Then, I gently peel it off the piece to reveal the red terra sig below.

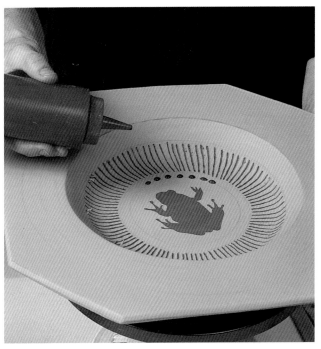

5. After allowing the terra sig to dry for about 30 minutes, I am able to draw with a pencil on the surface (the indentation will show later, but the graphite burns off). Following the circular pattern of the piece, I draw radiating lines outward toward the edge. These will give a guideline for the next application step.

7. Using a squeeze bottle filled with black slip, I draw beside and over the white incised lines created by sgraffito, using the bottle as if it were my brush. As you can see in the finished piece, I continued using sgraffito and slip trailing to further elaborate the center and edge of the piece.

6. Using a sgraffito tool, I scratch into the surface of the white slip to reveal the layer of red terra sig below. This is done with even movements of the tool from the inside toward the edge of the piece. Finding the right point of dryness at which to do sgraffito comes with experience.

CHAIR CHARGER
Slips and Cutouts

APPLICATIONS/MATERIALS

Leather-hard earthenware
   charger
White slip
Brushes
Brown terra sig

Paper cutouts of chairs, crowns,
   and other shapes
Small sponge
Black slip

1. To begin this demonstration, I'm applying a white slip to a leather-hard charger form with a hakeme brush, starting in the center and working out toward the edge. I stop at the line where the edge meets the bowl of the charger. Notice that the consistency of the slip is thick and creamy, creating smooth coverage. This white background will serve as an important part of my design later.

3. Meanwhile, I've prepared cutouts of four chairs that are all different but approximately the same size, making it possible for me to place one in each quarter of the bowl's center. I've dipped them in water and then pressed them on with my fingers. Fortunately, it's possible to move cutouts around if you don't hit the spot exactly the first time. Just lift them, adjust them, and dampen again with a paintbrush. Now I'm beginning to fill in one of the segments of my quartered design by painting over the first chair with brown terra sig.

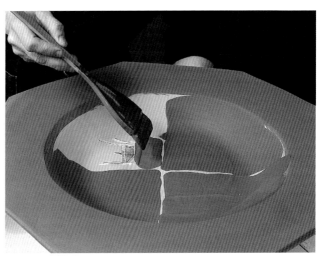

2. Here, I'm adding a coat of brown terra sig on the rim of the piece, keeping it as clean as possible where it meets the edge of the bowl. Later, I'll be able to touch up the edge, so a perfect line isn't necessary here.

4. Here, you can see the completed segments of brown terra sig (which I did first so I wouldn't have to change brushes) Again, I'm not obsessive about making com-

pletely neat lines where segments meet each other because I'll be creating a finished line later with another coat of slip.

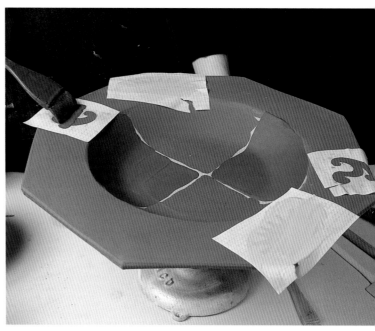

6. I've finished painting the two white cutout images, and now I'm using a contrasting black slip to paint over the remaining two.

5. Next I'll be using a masking technique. After the last coat of terra sig is dry enough to touch, I begin to use paper cutouts that are made by cutting the image from the paper and using what is left (I call this a negative cutout). Cutting into the surrounding paper to clip out the image creates a seam that can either be taped together on top before using the cutout or carefully hidden by lining up the edges when placing the paper on the piece. After several of the cutouts are placed around the rim, I begin painting over one of them with white slip.

7. As you can see, I've added more detail with negative cutouts around the edge. Even though I decided ahead on the images that I would use here, some of the placement of them has been purely improvisational. Many times, as a painter would do when choosing where to put the next stroke, I play around with various configurations until the design feels right. Here, I'm pulling up the last of the cutouts after the slips have dried, including the chairs that were placed in the center, revealing images that are like reliefs on the piece. After pulling the paper up, I sometimes have to touch up the edges of the designs with a small paintbrush and slip since the stencil can leave a blurry edge.

8. To give the chairs more texture, I'm using a sponging technique with a little bit of contrasting slip. I'm holding a couple of paintbrushes in preparation for painting outlines and details on top of the images I've stenciled.

9. Next, I'm painting white slip around the edges of the segments with a calligraphy brush to delineate the boundaries of the design. (This sort of brush holds a lot of paint and works well for this purpose.) Notice that this piece has become an exercise in contrasts between light and dark as I play one against the other.

10. I'm beginning to put the final touches on here as I outline and continue to define the shapes that I've stenciled. In the final piece you can see that I continued this process in freehand strokes until I was satisfied with the design.

LEAF CHARGER
Slips, Cutouts, and Sgraffito

APPLICATIONS/MATERIALS

Leather-hard earthenware
   charger
Brushes
Red terra sig
Paper cutouts

Dark blue slip
Blue slip
Sgraffito tool
Plastic squeeze bottle

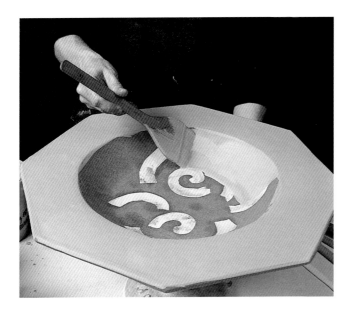

1. Because we've covered the basics of using stencils in the previous two exercises, I'm showing this piece at a more advanced point in the first photo. I've already applied a base coat of terra sig to leather-hard clay, placed cutouts on top of the coat after it dried, and am now painting a coat of dark blue slip on top of the cutouts.

3. I've added another layer of leaf-shaped stencils on top of the blue slip. I'm spattering terra sig around it with a paintbrush by plucking it from the top to the bottom (a technique called "fake airbrushing"). Notice that I've made use of the nice contrast that exists between the blue and red tints, playing a warm color against a cool one.

2. Yet another layer of stencils has been applied on top of the dark blue layer. Now I'm painting a layer of blue slip on top of all of this that will fill the bowl of the piece and leave the rim turquoise. So far, I've created layers of the following: red terra sig, stencils, dark blue slip, stencils, and the beginnings of light blue slip.

4. Next, I remove the leaf stencils with a matt knife, revealing the blue below and leaving a silhouette of my image.

8. I'm brushing terra sig over another leaf cutout on top of the layered design that I've revealed.

5-7. These steps show me carefully removing one layer of stencils after the next, trying not to pull off more than one at a time! This requires patient probing with the matt knife to find out which layer is next, since you'll be looking only at a flat slipped surface under which the stencils are hidden. It helps to keep a record of color, then layer, then color, during the process of layering so you can tell later what you're excavating.

9. To finish the edge of the piece, I've placed leaf cutouts on top of the dark blue slip and then painted an oval motif of terra sig on top of each. After the terra sig dries, I can remove the last stencils to reveal more images which echo the design inside.

10. To add finishing touches to my design, some of which I've again improvised, I'm scratching through the slip with a sgraffito tool to reveal layers of various colors beneath.

11. Continuing with the sgraffito technique, I've discovered a nice way to delineate the veins of the leaves, revealing a variety of colors underneath from the many layers that I've created with slips.

12. Now I'm scratching lines onto the edge of the charger, and you can see how the slip curls as I use the sgraffito tool.

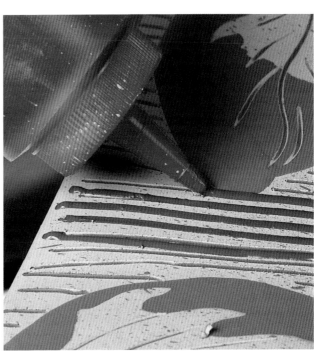

13. Using a squeeze bottle, I'm trailing slip into the gouges that I've created with the sgraffito tool. I continue this finishing touch around the rim of the piece.

TEACUP CHARGER
Commercial Underglaze Products and Cutouts

APPLICATIONS/MATERIALS

Bisque earthenware charger
Brushes
Cutouts
Soft graphite pencil

Assortment of commercial underglaze products including pencils, markers, chalks, crayons, watercolors in pan, and jars of underglaze color

1. Notice that the charger I'm using is white instead of brown. This is because I'm beginning this demonstration on bisqueware which has been fired with a coat of white slip. I'll be using commercial underglaze products for my design. All of these products, such as pencils, chalks, and watercolors, are foodsafe after the piece is glaze fired. Here, I'm tracing with a soft graphite pencil around a cutout of a teacup, simply holding the pattern in place with my hand. I've already drawn out the basics of the design that I plan to undertake with other stencils and a pencil.

3. Next, I've switched to a green underglaze pencil to add to my design. Doing this is just like drawing and painting on paper—if you have a variety of pencils and markers at your disposal, you can create any design that you can think of on bisqueware.

2. Using a black underglaze pencil, I fill in the details of the cup, using the image that I traced as a guide.

4. Now I'm adding a new form of underglaze by using a cobalt blue marker. This color will darken when the piece is fired.

5. I've switched to yet another wondrous underglaze product—the crayon. I'm filling in the background of part of my design, using expressionistic strokes that retain the character of the crayon. The crayon has a chalk-like feel to it on the surface of the bisqueware, almost like pastels on paper.

7. I'm using pink underglaze color from a jar to continue painting my design around the edge of the charger. These paints have the consistency of watercolors and are absorbed quickly into the porous surface of the bisqueware.

6. The pan that I'm holding here is full of semi-moist underglaze watercolors that I'm painting on to delineate a design I created with a stencil. Notice how placing the blue underglaze paint next to the brown crayon creates contrast between textures as well as warmth and coolness.

8. Now you can see that I've spent time adding details on the rim of the piece using underglaze pencils and crayons, creating an elaborate pattern. Furthermore, I'm continuing to add outlines to my forms with a black underglaze pencil. This piece uses a variety of underglaze products, but, of course, you can pick and choose which ones you want to combine. Your choices for drawing and painting are unlimited with this medium.

WINE GOBLET CHARGER
Maiolica Colors and Sgraffito

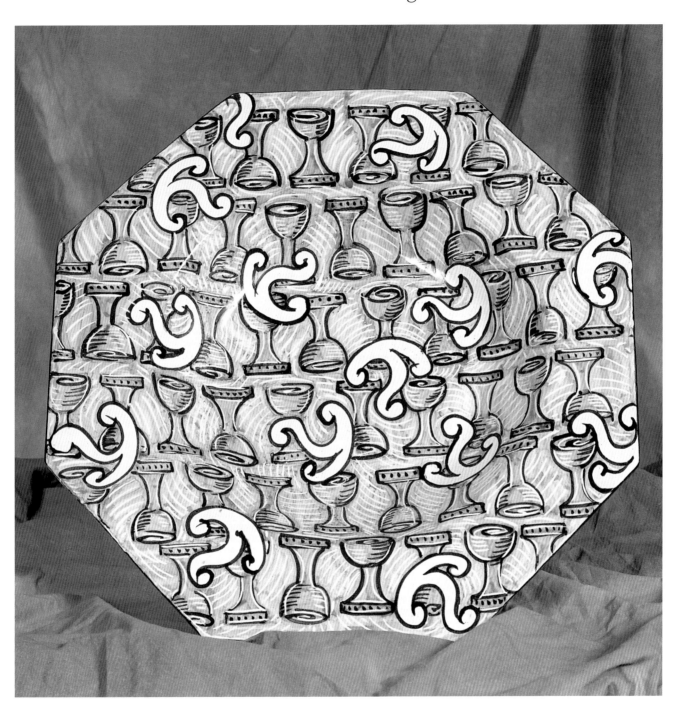

APPLICATIONS/MATERIALS

*Bisque earthenware
charger coated with
white maiolica glaze
Brushes
Ruler*

*Soft graphite pencil
Cutouts
Green and purple maiolica
colors (paints)
Sgraffito tool*

1. The white charger that you see here has been covered with a coat of maiolica glaze that has dried. I'm using a ruler and pencil to create horizontal divisions that are the width of a goblet-shaped cutout I've chosen.

3. Now I'm adding another template to the design, layering the image improvisationally on top of the structured design that I've created with the goblets.

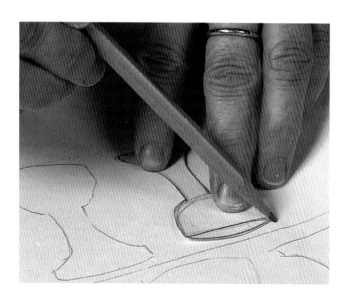

2. I'm tracing around the goblet cutout inside of the divisions that I've drawn, reversing the image across the expanse of the section to make an interlocking design.

4. I begin painting background sections of my design with green maiolica color, leaving the outlines of the cutout images white.

5. I'm undertaking the careful process of painting the goblets with purple maiolica color, leaving the other forms white.

6. The outlines of the shapes on the rim are articulated with a slender calligraphy brush and black maiolica color.

7. I'm continuing to outline images on the inside of the charger.

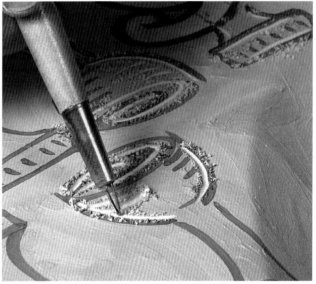

8-9. I'm using a sgraffito tool to scratch more lines on top of the images, creating shading and definition with white lines. The maiolica glaze shows through from underneath. After the piece is fired, the maiolica glaze and colors will perform their magic in the kiln, melding and darkening to create a dramatic surface.

PORTRAIT CHARGER
Commercial Underglaze Products

APPLICATIONS/MATERIALS

Bisque earthenware
charger
Photograph
Soft graphite pencil

Potter's pen
Underglaze crayon, pens, paints
Brushes
Dental tool or matt knife

1. Using a photograph as a guide, I draw a cameo interpretation on the white bisqued surface of the charger's center with a potter's pen.

2. Here, I'm giving more definition to my drawing using a black underglaze pencil to fill out details.

3. At this stage, I'm stippling (creating small dots with the end of my potter's pen) the background behind the portrait.

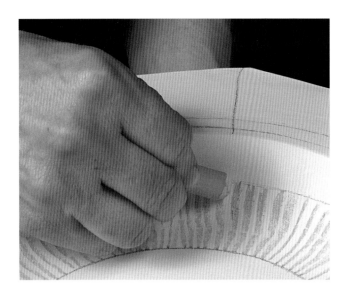

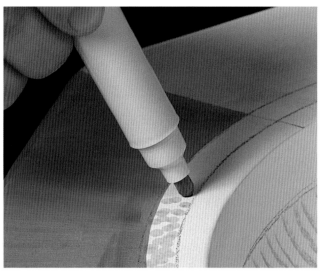

4. Surrounding this circular image I've drawn a radiating design which I'm tracing over a with a blue underglaze crayon. As with the previous pieces, I'm creating a symmetrical design using the natural form of the bowl of the piece. This is made easier by turning the banding wheel as I'm making the marks.

6. I'm using a marker again to stipple around the inside edge of the charger, filling in an area that I've already drawn out with a marker.

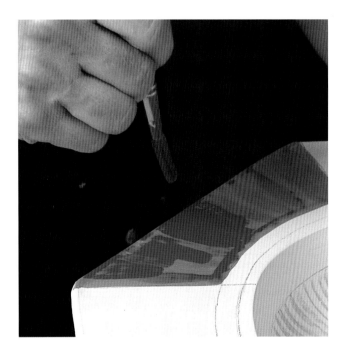

5. I'm now painting the edge of the charger with blue underglaze paint. Notice how it absorbs into the bisqueware like watercolor, remaining somewhat transparent. Another coat of this color added later will make it appear more opaque, as you see from the photo of the finished piece.

7. To create a band of red underglaze paint around the inside edge, I poise a long calligraphy brush and turn the banding wheel slowly to create an even line. The touch of the brush is light, not heavy: this is something that you'll need to practice to perfect. Using the wheel makes it possible to get even coverage and a consistent line.

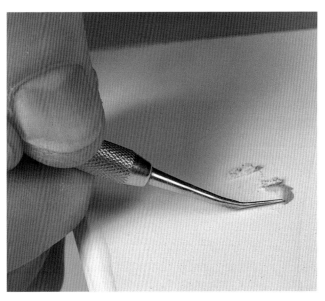

8. Now I'm adding more red to the outside rim, which is divided into eight sections. I use a long steady brush stroke to create each straight line needed and then use the banding wheel to proceed to the next section of the rim.

10. I've dropped a spot of red paint onto the white surface while painting. After it has dried, I can scrape it off to correct the mistake with a dental tool or matt knife.

9. I'm putting the final touches on my design by tracing the dividing lines of the eight sections I created using the natural lines of the charger's edge.

PATTERNED CHARGER
Decals

APPLICATIONS/MATERIALS

Glazed earthenware charger
Screen from artwork
Triple beam balance scale
Mixing medium for overglaze
  enamels colorants
Overglaze enamel/China
  paint powdered colorants
Spatula
Mortar and pestle

Squeegee
Decal paper
Polyurethane varnish
Acetone or paint thinner
Scissors
Paper towels
Brush
Overglaze enamel paint

1. To begin the process of creating a decal, we'll be making a print from a screen first. Here, I'm using a triple beam balance scale to weigh out liquid medium to mix with enamel powder to make the "ink" for printing (Remember that the usual ratio of medium to colorant is two to one.) I transfer the medium, using a spatula, into a mortar and then wash out the scale's measuring container.

3. The two are ground together using the pestle, rolling it on the sides of the mortar to crush and dissolve the powder. I continue doing this until the powder is totally blended, and the colorant, which will serve as the "ink," has a thick cottage cheese consistency.

2. I'm weighing out half the amount of powdered colorant on the scale and adding this to the medium.

4. Wearing protective gloves, I've transferred the ink to the screen with a spatula in preparation for printing. I have paper and a squeegee ready for this process.

117

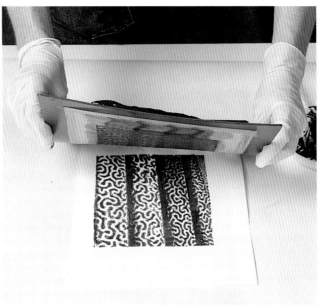

5. Next, I have carefully placed the screen on the decal paper and positioned the rubber end of the squeegee at the top of the screen in preparation for printing. (I recommend always doing a trial run to test the image and hone your technique.)

7. Now I'm pulling the print away from the screen, revealing my design on the paper. The print must be allowed to dry.

6. Now you can see that I've used a quick, even, and firm movement to drag the squeegee across the screen, dispersing the ink through the mesh and printing an image. (You'll have to press very hard to do this, so roll up your sleeves!)

8. I'm painting a coat of polyurethane varnish with a wide brush onto the print (the brush will have to be cleaned with acetone or paint thinner after use and then washed with soap). The varnish will create a film on the decal paper and print when it dries.

9. I've measured the width of the rim of the charger and am now cutting four equal-sized strips of the print which will fit around the edge. I've also placed the charger on a banding wheel in preparation for later applying the decals.

11. After removing the paper strips from the water, I have gently coaxed the printed image off one of the strips and applied it. I'm careful not to tear it in this process. You see me positioning another decal on the edge of the piece. I'll gently rub it on, being careful to squeeze out air bubbles as I go. After blotting the surface dry with paper towels, I can add color to the surface with overglaze enamels.

10. I'm submerging the decals in a bowl of water where they will soak for a few minutes until they begin to lift off the surface of the paper (the ink has now bonded with the varnish).

12. To complete the piece, I'm using black and red overglaze enamel paint that I've squeezed from tubes into a plastic palette box to further decorate the piece on top of the decals.

The question is not what you look at, but what you see.

-Henry David Thoreau

INSPIRATION AND FINDING YOUR OWN VOICE

Where does creativity begin?

Of course it begins within the individual, a spark that could light a roaring fire. But in order to create a physical manifestation in the world, the idea must get out of your head. Creativity must materialize in time and space, and for this to happen you must take action.

Fear stops us from creating work we have within us. This often happens as we criticize the germ of inception. You must allow yourself to dwell in the process, to make mistakes, to stand in the place of not knowing, to generate from nothing.

As children learning to walk, we fall again and again, laughing and crying, not knowing how to walk, but inventing it as we go along. As adults, we have to give up our attachment to preconceived notions of what we are doing, and move forward in spite of not always knowing everything about something that we dream of undertaking.

Detach from the end product. No matter how much eventual finesse you may acquire, there will be some good pieces, some not so good. Stay focused on each aspect of your daily practice of making art, whether it be material manipulation, research, sharing your processes with others, or cleaning the studio. If nothing else, ceramics will teach you detachment through the haphazard luck of the kiln.

Love it. Work all the time so that things can happen when you least expect them. Be conscious and fully attuned to what is happening while you work. That is where the magic of making art manifests itself. Like music or dance, creating forces you into being fully alive, fully in the moment. The final object will eventually become acceptable to you; although, personally, I'm always more excited about the piece I haven't made yet.

Copy. Imitate. Borrow. Look everywhere all the time. Be influenced. Figure out what you like and what is good about it. Collect the things that you love (in museums, in fashion, in film, on your refrigerator). Then begin. You'll create your own unique brew from what you begin to imagine and create, while ideas evolve and take on a life of their own. This cannot be a conscious effort, or predictable, or controllable. It has its own tempo.

All of these images that inspire you become aspects of your visual vocabulary. It's like learning a foreign language. We learn a few words and word by word we build sentences, gather paragraphs, and eventually tell stories. Your visual vocabulary gradually communicates your own mythology.

Constantly study. I recently saw a show of Degas' paintings at the Metropolitan Museum of Art. Included in this show was his vast personal collection of artwork by artists he admired. Most memorable of all were the studies of the masters from the Louvre that he made until the final years of his life, long after he was an established and acknowledged artist. Degas' example is a good reminder for us.

Know when to stop. Cook. Exercise. Read. Clean the house. Sleep late. Be with other people. Nourish your soul. Burn out happens to artists too.

Share. Share. Share. Talk about your work, show it to whoever will look at it. Find other people who make stuff. Have shows together. Getting your work out to the community is the last step of completing your work. Don't stop until you do. This will feed you and give you and your work a place in the world.

Learning to make pots is like learning to write. When as children we were being taught to write they didn't tell us the great thing to aim at was to make the writing "express our personality"; personality is something too big and too mysterious to be treated that way. They taught us skill, or craftsmanship, that is, to make our writing legible. But while you are learning to write legibly your handwriting becomes yours and only yours. Legibility is not going to rob it of its personality; on the contrary, it makes it possible for your personality to flower and be seen; your handwriting is you and nobody else can imitate it exactly.

The best way to impart character and personality to pots is to first turn your attention to other matters; to make them with as much concentration as you are capable of, to enlarge your skill over as wide a range as possible, to get to know your materials by living with them, trying to understand them, and finding out little by little—not with your head but with your body—how they want to be treated; in fact, to treat them with proper respect as we would a friend. Then, nothing can stop your personality from appearing in your pots. They will be as individual and unmistakable as your handwriting. But the handwriting has to be legible; if it isn't, the message—the meaning—will not be communicated.

-Michael Cardew from *A Potter's Companion: Imagination, Originality, and Craft* by Ronald Larson

▲ **CARY ESSER** (Kansas City, Missouri), *Sarracenia Duet*, 8 x 8 x 1" (20 x 20 x 2.5 cm), 1996. Red earthenware. Press-molded tile (bas relief). Terra sigillata, glazes. Δ04 firing. Photo by Seth Tice-Lewis.

◄ **LYNN PETERS** (Chicago, Illinois), *Urn*, 15" height (37.5 cm), 1997. Press-molded earthenware. Terra sigillata, sgraffito. Δ04 firing. Photo by Jeff Martin.

◄ **BEVERLY CRIST** (Dallas, Texas), *Jack of Diamonds*, 22.25 x 11.5 x 6.5 (55.6 x 28.8 x 16.3 cm), 1997. White earthenware. Slab construction. Underglaze and glaze, underglaze watercolor and pencil, clear glaze. Δ1 bisque firing. Δ04 glaze firing.
Photo by Tracy Hicks.

◄ **NAO T. TAJIRI** (Portland, Oregon), *Random Order*, 16 x 13.5" (40 x 34 cm), 1998. Red earthenware. Handbuilt. Slips. Engobes. Underglazes. Δ04 firing. Photo by Steven J. Scardina.

▲ **Lisa Orr** Lisa Orr (Austin, Texas), ***Teapot***, 7 x 8.5 x 6"
(17.5 x 21.25 x 15 cm), 1996. Wheel thrown.
Earthenware. Sprigged clay. Terra sigillata, slips, glazes.
Δ03 firing. Courtesy of Ferrin Gallery, Northhampton, MA.

▲ **Lisa M. Naples** (Doylestown,
Pennsylvania), ***Teapot***, 7 x 9 x 6"
(17.5 x 22.5 x 15 cm), 1998. Slip
cast. Slips, glazes. Δ04 firing

◄ **Deborah Black** (Toronto,
Canada), ***Rasberry Leaf Platter***,
16.5 x 11 x 2" (41.3 x 27.5 x
5 cm), 1993. Earthenware.
Slips, glazes. Δ04 firing.

▶ **GAIL KENDALL** (Lincoln, Nebraska), *Tureen*, 13 x 13 x 10" (32.5 x 32.5 x 25 cm), 1996. Terra cotta. Coiled, paddled, scraped. Underglaze on greenware, glazes, 24K gold luster. Δ07 bisque firing. Δ04 glaze firing. Photo by Roger Bruhn.

▼ **KERRI BUXTON, BRAD TAYLOR** (Salt Lake City, Utah), *Elaborate Teapot*, 11" height (27.5 cm), 1997. White earthenware. Handbuilt. Alkaline glazes. Δ03-05 firing.

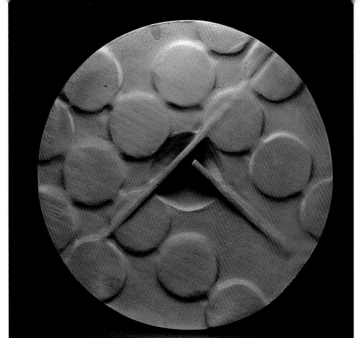

◄ **MARGARET RATTLE**
(Sebastopol, California),
Alamosa Aerial-5, 20 x 20 x 3"
(50 x 50 x 7.5 cm), 1997. Slab
clay. Thrown. Sprayed slip,
mason stain, lithium, and other
materials. Δ01 bisque firing.
Δ06 glaze firing. Photo by artist.

◄ **CARRIE ANNE PARKS**
(Riverdale, Michigan), *Puppet
Theater with Garlands*, 14.5 x
11 x 6.75" (36.3 x 27.5 x 16.8
cm), Earthenware. Slab-built and
pinched with press-molded and
modeled relief decoration.
Underglazes. Δ06 bisque firing.
Δ04 refiring. Photo by artist.

▲ **BRIAN HIVELY** (Cook, Minnesota), *Swirl*, 31 x 24 x 8" (77.5 x 60 x 20 cm), 1997. Earthenware. Handbuilt using coils. Textured glazes, underglazes, slips. Δ04 firings.
Photo by Anne Boudreau.

▶ **HO-JEONG JEONG** (Rochester, New York), *Frozen Water*, 35 x 20 x 16" (87.5 x 50 x 40 cm), 1996. Earthenware. Coil built. Airbrushed with underglazes. Clear glaze. Δ04 firing.
Photo by Jinhwan Kim.

◄ **VIRGINIA SCOTCHIE**
(Columbia, South Carolina), **Red Stack**, 22 x 18 x 20" (55 x 45 x 50 cm), 1994. Earthenware. Coil pinched. Rings made from plaster mold. Glazes. Δ04 firing. Δ019 enamel glaze firing. Photo by Hunter Clarkson.

▼ **PRISCILLA HOLLINGSWORTH**
(Augusta, Georgia), **Four Flanged Forms**, 22 x 36 x 36" (55 x 90 x 90 cm), 1996. Terra cotta. Handbuilt with slab and coil. Δ04 oxidation firing. Photo by artist.

▲ **ANDREA GILL** (Alfred, New York), *Penelope's Dilemma: Blue Series II*, 18 x 12 x 5" (45 x 30 x 12.5 cm), 1997. Press mold with coil additions. Terra sigillata, copper glaze. Δ05 bisque firing.

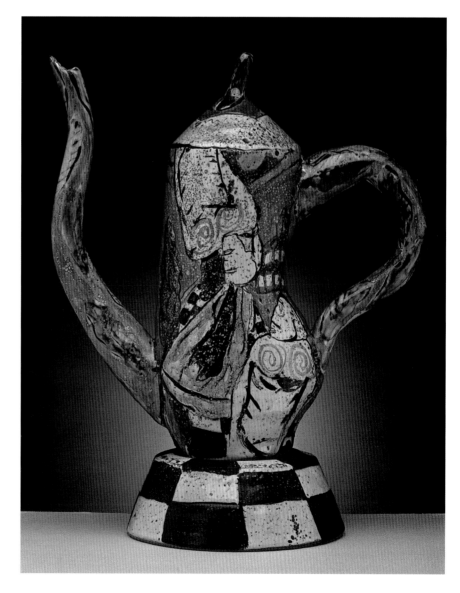

▶ **DEBORAH GROOVER** (Monticello, Florida), *Tuscan Dreamscape*, 15 x 10 x 6" (37.5 x 25 x 15 cm), 1995. Earthenware. Handbuilt. Maiolica. Δ04 firing. Courtesy of Ferrin Gallery, Northhampton, MA.

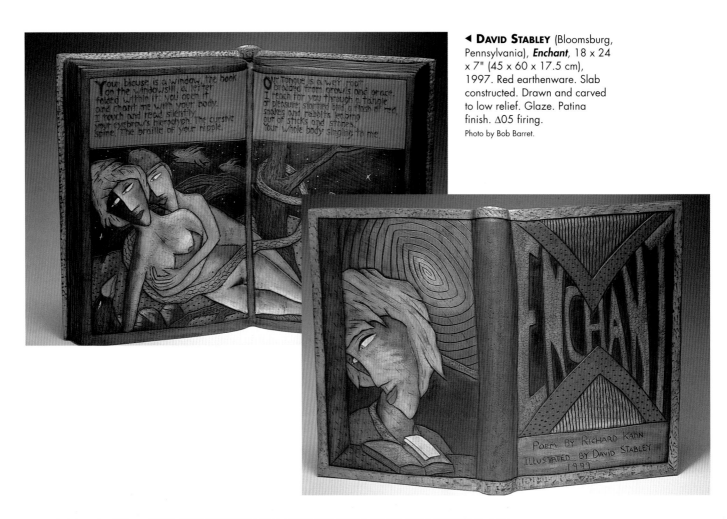

◄ **DAVID STABLEY** (Bloomsburg, Pennsylvania), *Enchant*, 18 x 24 x 7" (45 x 60 x 17.5 cm), 1997. Red earthenware. Slab constructed. Drawn and carved to low relief. Glaze. Patina finish. Δ05 firing.
Photo by Bob Barret.

◄ **MARK JOHNSON** (South Portland, Maine), *Platter*, 3 x 22 x 22" (7.5 x 55 x 55 cm), 1997. Red earthenware. Formed over plaster hump mold. Red terra sigillata and black cracking slip. Δ04 firing. Photo by artist.

▲ **ANDREA GILL** (Alfred, New
York), *Embroidered Layers*, 46 x
21 x 11" (115 x 52.5 x 27.5
cm), 1996. Slab built using
pressmolds and handbuilding.
Slips applied with brushes and
stencils. Clear glaze applied
with toothbrush. Δ03 firing. Δ07
bisque firing.

▲ **KATHY TRIPLETT**
(Weaverville, North
Carolina), *Tall Tea*, 29 x 12 x
11" (72.5 x 30 x 27.5 cm),
1998. Brown earthenware.
Handbuilt with slab. Extruded.
Terra sigillata. Glaze over black
copper oxide wash. Δ05 firing.
Photo by Tim Barnwell.

◄ **CHRISTINE FEDERIGHI** (Coral Gables, Florida), *Charms and Amulets*, 72 x 8 x 5" (180 x 20 x 12.5 cm), 1996. Stoneware clay. Coil built and carved. Oil patination. Sealed. Δ05-04 firing. Photo by Fareed Al Mashat.

▼ **PATRICK DOUGHERTY** (Penland, North Carolina), *Ventilator*, 24 x 7.5" (60 x 18.8 cm), 1997. White earthenware. Wheel formed. Underglazes on bone dry. Slip trailing. Glaze. Δ03 bisque firing. Δ05 glaze firing. Photo by Tom Mills.

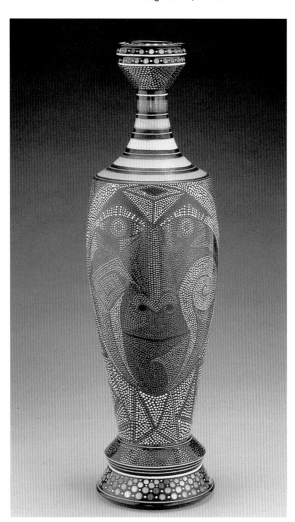

► **Antonio Fink**
(Philadelphia, Pennsylvania),
Red (from The Four Seasons),
1.2 yd x 17.6" x 2" (1.10m x
44cm x 5cm), 1997. Raku clay.
160 hand-cut tiles using a
wooden stencil. Commercial
underglazes and glazes. Δ06
firing. Photo by John Carlano.

▼ **Cheryl Tall** (Stuart, Florida),
Magister Operis, 35 x 16 x 17"
(87.5 x 40 x 42.5 cm), 1998.
Earthenware. Coil-built in sections with inner flanges. Slip and
studio-made glazes. Δ04 firing.
Photo by Mark Taylor.

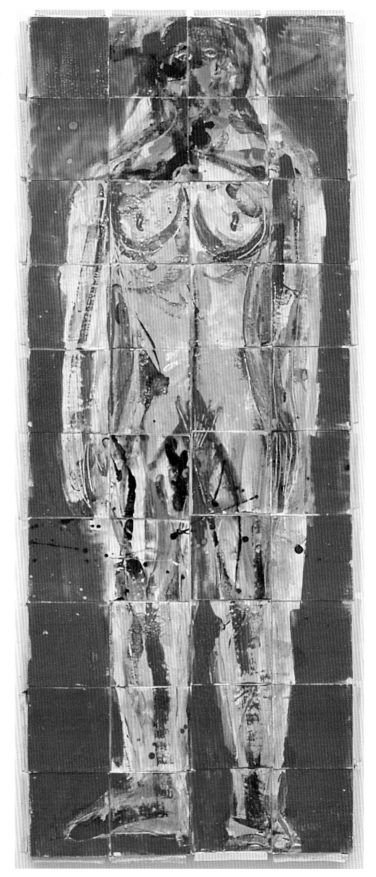

APPENDICES

Appendix I

Red Earthenware Clay
Cone 06-01

Red Art Clay	50%
Gold Art Clay	15%
Fire Clay	10%
Talc	10%
Nepheline Syenite	10%
Old Mine #4 or Kentucky ball clay	5%
Frit 3124	2%
Barium	1%
Grog	5-10%

Appendix II

Old Reliable Slip (white base)
Cone 06-03

Old Mine #4 or Kentucky ball clay	40%
Edgar's Plastic Kaolin	20%
Nepheline Syenite	10%
Talc	15%
Flint	15%
Add colorants at	15%

Appendix III

Terra Sigillata
Cone 06-03

3 cups (720 mL) water
400 grams Red Art Clay
3-7 drops Darvon #7 or sodium silicate

Appendix IV

White Terra Sigillata
Cone 06-03

3 cups (720 mL) water
400 g Old Mine #4 or Kentucky ball clay
3-7 drops of Darvon # 7 (or sodium silicate deflocculant)

Appendix V

Hands in Clay Cone 05 Glaze Recipe
Cone 06-03

Frit # 3195	88%
Edgar's Plastic Kaolin	10%
Bentonite	2%

Appendix VI

Birdsall-Worthington Clear
Cone 06-03

Gerstley Borate	55%
Edgar's Plastic Kaolin	30%
Flint	15%

Appendix VII

Matthias' Maiolica
Cone 06-03

Frit #3124	83.34%
Old Mine #4 or Kentucky ball clay	8.33%
Edgar's Plastic Kaolin	8.33%
plus Zircopax	11.11%

Appendix VIII

Arbuckle Maiolica
Cone 06-03

Frit#3124	65.75%
F-4 Feldspar	17.24%
Edgar's Plastic Kaolin	10.82%
Nepheline Syenite	6.24%
Tin oxide	5%
Zircopax	10%
Bentonite	2%

Appendix IX

Coloring Oxides

Cobalt Carbonate	.5-1%	medium to strong blue
Copper Carbonate	1-2%	light to strong green
Iron Oxide	2-6%	tan to dark reddish brown
Manganese Carbonate	4-6%	medium to dark purple
Chrome Oxide	2%	green
Rutile	5%	tan
Nickle Oxide	2%	gray or brown
Iron Chromate	2%	gray
Vanadium Stain	6%	medium yellow

From *Hands in Clay: An Introduction to Ceramics, Third Edition* by Charlotte F. Speight and John Toki. Copyright ©1995, 1989 by Mayfield Publishing Company. Reprinted by permission of the publisher.

APPENDICES

Appendix X

Cone-Firing Ranges

The ranges below are for large Orton and Seger cones, fired at a temperature rise of 270°F (132°C) per hour. Note that the temperature at which a cone will melt will vary depending on the rate of temperature rise in the firing.

Orton	Seger	Degrees F	Degrees C
022		1112	605
021		1137	615
020		1175	635
019		1261	683
	019	1265	685
	018	1301	705
018		1323	717
	017	1346	730
017		1377	747
	016	1391	755
	015a	1436	780
016		1458	792
015		1479	804
014		1540	838
013		1566	852
012		1623	884
011		1641	894
010		1661	905
09		1693	923
	09a	1751	935
08	08a	1751	955
	07a	1778	970
07		1784	984
	06a	1803	990
06		1830	999
	05a	1832	1000
	04a	1847	1025
05		1915	1046
	03a	1931	1055
04		1940	1060
	02a	1955	1085
03		2014	1101
	01a	2021	1105
02		2048	1120
	1a	2057	1125
01		2079	1137
	2a	2102	1150
1		2109	1154
2		2124	1162
3		2134	1168
	3a	2138	1170
4		2167	1186
	4a	2183	1195
5		2185	1196
	5a	2219	1215
6		2232	1222
7	6a	2264	1240
	7	2300	1260
8		2305	1263
9	8	2336	1280
	9	2372	1300
10		2381	1305
11		2399	1315
	10	2408	1320
12		2419	1326
	11	2444	1340
13		2455	1346

GLOSSARY

Alumina. An extremely hard mineral that is added to ceramic glazes to strengthen and harden them due to its resistance to high temperatures. These chemical characteristics prevent excessive running of glazes on the surface of the clay during firing.

Banding wheel. A revolving stand, similar to a "lazy Susan," which sculptors and ceramicists use to slowly turn work while applying glazes or decorations.

Bat. A plaster, wood, or plastic disc which ceramicists use to transport pottery around the studio and to the kiln.

Bisque firing. A preliminary firing of ware which removes all moisture from the piece and provides a more stable form with which to work when applying decorations and glazes.

Bone dry. The stage of clay dryness at which the clay has been air-dried until it is as dry as possible prior to firing. Terra sigillata is often applied at the bone dry stage of dryness.

Carbonates. Carbonized chemical compounds that act as coloring agents in clay, glazes, and slips.

Ceramics. The art of making objects out of clay derived from the Greek word "keramos" which indicated a large Athenian depository of clay.

Clay body. A mixture of natural clay and other structurally compatible materials that make the clay workable and ideal for firing at certain temperatures.

Colorants. Chemical combinations (oxides and carbonates) which are used to color clays and glazes.

Crawling. A glaze flaw which is characterized by peeling off of the surface of the ware.

Crazing. A glaze flaw that resembles a spider's web of cracks over the surface of the ware.

Decal. A visual reproduction of an image that is temporarily adhered onto a special paper until removed and fired onto ware as a surface decoration. Decals are fired at low temperatures and are usually used on smooth glazed pieces.

GLOSSARY

Deflocculant. A material such as sodium silicate or sodium carbonate which reduces the amount of water needed to make slip fluid—consequently reducing shrinkage after it is applied to the clay.

Earthenware. A low-fire blend of clay used worldwide for domestic ware which is usually red and porous.

Fit. The act of clay and surface components shrinking at a similar rate.

Flux. A substance that lowers the melting point of clay bodies or glazes.

Frit. A glaze that has been melted and reground to a powdered state that renders it more stable and less toxic. Frits are used as fluxes in glazes and some clays. Feldspar is a natural frit.

Glaze. A substance composed primarily of silica that creates a glassy coating that is fused onto the surface of the clay when fired. Glazes may be matte or glossy, depending on their components.

Glaze firing. The kiln firing that produces a vitrified or mature glaze melt.

Greenware. Any unfired clay object, whether leather hard or bone dry.

Grog. Fired clay particles with larger sizes which serve to "open" a clay body and therefore reduce shrinkage, cracking, and warping. Grog also helps the clay body to dry.

Heat soaking. The process of keeping a kiln at a constant temperature for a certain amount of time, which helps to create a smoother surface on ceramic pieces by allowing trapped gases to escape and by allowing the glaze time to heal over after it bubbles up when melting.

High fire. The range of firing from cone 2 up to cone 10 or 13. Ware fired at cone 2 and up is usually referred to as stoneware.

Kaolinite. The geological name for clay—a naturally occurring mineral created by the disintegration of feldspathic rock.

Kiln. A container or furnace used for firing ceramics.

Leather hard. The stage of clay dryness at which the clay is dry enough to retain fingermarks, but still wet enough to be carved or joined. At this stage, much of the moisture has evaporated and shrinkage has just ended. Slips are often applied at the leather hard stage of dryness, and this stage is ideal for sgraffito.

Low fire. The range of firing ware that is usually between cone 015 and cone 1. Ware fired at low temperatures is usually referred to as earthenware.

Maiolica. A type of eathenware technique that became popular in thirteenth century Italy after being introduced by the Spanish. Maiolica ware is created by applying an opaque, matte glaze on an unfired piece. After this step colorants are painted on top before both layers are fired and fused together to create a bright, colorful surface known as maiolica glaze.

Maturation point (or maturity). The firing point at which a particular clay body reaches its maximum hardness and nonporosity.

Opacifier. A chemical compound added to a glaze to create opacity, or the state of not permitting light to pass through the surface.

Overglaze enamels/China paints. Colored paint-like surface decorations that are applied on top of a previously fired and glazed piece which is then fired again at low temperatures.

Oxidation firing. A firing process that takes place in an atmosphere where there is an ample supply of oxygen in the kiln chamber to guarantee that complete combustion of the contents can occur. This atmosphere contains enough oxygen to allow the metals in clays and glazes to produce their oxide colors. Electric kilns naturally produce oxidizing firings unless reducing materials are added. Bright, clear, low-fire colors are associated with glazes and clays fired in an oxidation atmosphere.

Oxide. A combination of an element with oxygen. In ceramics, oxides are added to clays, slips, and glazes as coloring agents. Firing produces the colors through their interaction with oxygen.

Peepholes. Holes in the wall or door of a kiln created to allow safe observation from outside. Peepholes also allow gases and heat to escape during the firing and cooling processes.

GLOSSARY

Pinholes. A glaze flaw consisting of small pores in the glaze surface that are caused by escaping gases.

Plasticity. The ability of damp clay to readily change shape without cracking.

Porcelain. A blend of clay, usually white, characteristically fired to a high temperature at which the clay body becomes vitrified and nonporous as well as translucent.

Pugging. The process by which clay is thoroughly mixed in a pug mill, which eliminates air bubbles.

Reduction firing. A firing process that takes place in an atmosphere that reduces the proportion of gas to oxygen, forcing the oxygen-starved flame to attack the oxides in the clay and glazes of the ware. Color changes occur during this process because insufficient oxygen is supplied to the kiln for complete combustion and carbon dioxide in the kiln combines with oxygen in the oxides of the clay body and glaze. This type of firing is associated with high-fire stoneware, porcelain, raku, and lusters.

Sgraffito. A surface decoration drawing technique in which coats of contrasting underglazes or colored slips are applied to clay in the leather-hard or bone-dry stages, and then scratched off with a fine-pointed tool to reveal layers beneath the surface. The process stems from an old ceramic drawing technique which began with the use of white slip over reddish clay which was scratched to reveal a crisp red line.

Silica. Found in nature as quartz or flint sand, this crystalline compound is used to manufacture glass and is the primary ingredient in ceramic glazes.

Slaking. The chemical change that occurs when a substance such as clay is combined with water.

Slip. A finely sieved mixture of clay and water, either white or colored, which can be applied to clay surfaces in one or more layers. Slips are used to create a neutral ground on which to apply surface decorations as well as alone as painted decorations.

Slip trailing. A method of decorating ware by squeezing slip from a bottle or nozzle onto the surface of the pottery to create raised lines.

Soaking. Maintaining a certain temperature in the kiln for a prescribed period of time in order to achieve heat saturation.

Stains. Commercially prepared and refined raw chemicals used for coloring clays and glazes. Stains are usually more reliable and stable than oxides when used for coloring.

Stoneware. A blend of clay, usually brownish in color, that is characteristically fired to a high temperature at which the clay body becomes vitrified and nonporous, but not translucent.

Terra sigillata. A variety of slip often nicknamed "terra sig" that is made by mixing a fine clay with water and allowing it to settle. Characteristically thinner than other slips, terra sig dries to a soft, silky sheen. This old method of decorating was orginally used by the Romans and later the Greeks to create an unglazed, shiny surface on earthenware.

Talc. A magnesium-bearing rock which acts as a flux and adds whiteness to a clay body.

Terra cotta. A type of clay whose names means translates as "baked earth" from Italian. Terra cotta that has been produced and used since ancient times and its name is often used interchangeably with earthenware.

Test tiles. Tiles used to test the clay body surface and planned decoration material prior to producing a kiln load of work.

Underglazes. Any colored agents, such as slips and commercial underglazes, which are used under a glaze. Today, the word underglaze most commonly indicates commercially made products colored with oxides and stains in bases formulated to decorate greenware and bisqueware with color before a protective glaze is applied. Underglazes may also be fired onto the surface without a protective glaze, creating a matte surface.

Vitrification. The point at which a clay body or glaze reaches a glassy, dense, hard, and nonabsorbent condition.

RESOURCES

Suppliers

American Art Clay Co, Inc.
4717 West 16th Street
Indianapolis, IN 46222
Ph (317)244-6871
Fax (317)248-9300

AMACO American Art Clay Co.
4717 West 16th Street
Indianapolis, IN 46222
Ph (800)374-1600

Ceramic Supply of New York and
New Jersey, Inc.
7 Rt. 46 West
Lodi, NJ 07644
Ph (973)340-3005
Fax (973)340-0089

Columbus Clay
1049 West Fifth Ave.
Columbus, OH 43212
Ph (614)294-1114

Ferro Frit Corporation Ceramics Division
P.O. Box 6550
Cleveland, OH
Ph (216)641-8580

Great Lakes Clay
120 So. Lincoln Ave.
Carpentersville, IL 60110
Ph (847)551-1070

Highwater Clays
238 Clingman Ave.
Asheville, NC 28801
Ph (828)252-6033

Frederickson Kiln Company
Alfred Station, NY 14803
Ph (607)587-9000

Mason Color Works
PO Box 76
East Liverpool, OH 43920
Ph (330)385-4400
Fax (330)385-4488

Minnesota Clay Company
8001 Grand Ave. South
Bloomington, MN 55420
Ph (800)252-9872
Ph (612)884-9101

O'Hommel Company
235 Hope Street
Carnegie, PA 15106
Ph (412)279-0700
Fax (412)279-1213

Skutt Ceramic Products
6441 Southeast Johnson Creek Blvd.
Portland, OR 97206
Ph (503)231-7726
Fax (503)774-7833

Standard Ceramic Supply CO
PO Box 4435
Pittsburgh, PA 15205
Ph (412)276-6333

Book Suppliers

Chester Book Company
4 Maple Street
Chester, CT 06412
Ph (860)526-9887

Lark Books
50 College Street
Asheville, NC 28801
Ph (828)253-0467
Fax (828)253-7952

The Potter's Shop
31 Thorpe Road
Needham Heights, MA 02494
Ph (781)449-7687
Fax (781)449-9098

RESOURCES

Periodicals

American Ceramics
9 East 45th Street
New York, NY 10017

Ceramics Art and Perception
35 William Street
Paddington, NSW 2021
Australia

Ceramics Monthly
1609 Northwest Blvd.
Columbus, OH 43212

Ceramic Review
21 Carnaby St.
London WIV IPH
United Kingdom

Ceramics Technical
35 William street
Paddington, NSW 2021
Australia

Clay Times
P.O Box 365
Waterford, VA 20197-0365

The Crafts Report
300 Water Street
Wilmington, DE 19801

Studio Potter
P.O. Box 70
Goffstown, NH 03045

Organizations

American Ceramic Society
735 Ceramic Place
P.O. Box 6136
Westerville, OH 43086

American Craft Council
72 Spring Street
New York, NY 10012-4019
Ph (212)274-0630

Craft Emergency Relief Fund
P.O. Box 838
Montpelier, VT 05601
(Emergency loans)

Friends of Terra Cotta
c/o Tunick
771 West End Ave.
New York, NY 10025

National Assembly of State Art Agencies
1010 Vermont Ave. N.W.
Suite 920
Washington DC 20005

NCECA, National Council for Education in the
Ceramic Arts
c/o Regina Brown
P.O. Box 1677
Bandon, OH 97411
Ph (800)996-2322

National Endowment for the Arts
1100 Pennsylvania Ave. NW
Washington DC 20506
(Grants)

Orton Firing Institute
P.O. Box 460
Westerville, OH 43081

Tile Heritage Foundation
PO Box 1850
Healdsburg, CA 95448

Tiles and Architectural Ceramics Books
3 Browns Rise, Buckland Common, TRING
Herts, HP23 6NJ, England

CONTRIBUTING ARTISTS

The following artists' works are shown on the pages listed after their names:

Lynn Peters (Chicago, IL), title page, contents page, 8, 10, 20, 25, 32, 59, 87, 92, 94, 95, 98, 102, 106, 112, 116, 122

Stanley Mace Andersen (Bakersville, CA), 57

Linda Arbuckle (Micanopy, FL), 55

Chuck Aydlett (St. Cloud, MN), 27

Posey Bacopoulos (New York, NY), 56, 89

Janet Belden (Long Island City, NY), 57, 91

Deborah Black (Toronto, Canada), 23, 92, 124

William Brouillard (Cleveland, OH), 27

Mark Burleson (Asheville, NC), 70

Kerri Buxton, Brad Taylor (Salt Lake City, UT), 125

Robin Campo (Chamblee, GA), 89

Jean Cappaadonna-Nichols (Tupelo, Missippi), 28

Michael Carlin (Burgettstown, PA), 65

Michel Louise Conroy (San Marcos, TX), 6, 21, 22, 81

Beverly Crist (Dallas, TX), 6, 123

Patrick Dougherty (Penland, NC), 86, 132

Melody Ellis (Philadelphia, PA), 22

Cary Esser (Kansas City, MO), 22, 80, 122

Anne Farley Gaines (Chicago, IL), 26

Christine Federighi (Coral Gables, FL), 132

Antonio Fink (Philadelphia, PA), 83, 133

Sharon Fliegelman (Topango, CA), 89

Verne Funk (San Antonio, TX), 71, 84

Carolyn Genders (West Sussex, Great Britain), 20

Andrea Gill (Alfred, New York), title page, 19, 88, 129, 131

Carol Gouthro (Seattle, WA), title page, 72, 74, 91

Deborah Groover (Monticello, FL), 129

Marylou Higgins (Pittsboro, NC), 75

Bryan Hively (Cook, MN), 19, 127

Priscilla Hollingsworth (Augusta, GA), 128

Linda Huey (Alfred Station, NY), 30, 90

Yoshiro Ikeda (Manhattan, KS), 90

Ho-Jeong Jeong (Rochester, NY), 127

Marcia Jestaedt (Bowie, MD), 73, 75

Erik Johanson (Tinton Falls, NJ), 23

Mark Johnson (South Portland, ME), 29, 88, 130

Gail Kendall (Lincoln, NE), 30, 125

Michael Kifer (Richland, MI), 86

James Klueg (Duluth, MN), 64

Karen Koblitz (Los Angeles, CA), 26

Cindy Kolodziejski (Venice, CA), 63

Anne Kraus (Boulder, CO), 24

Amy Kwong (Alberta, Canada), 64

Marc Leuthold (Potsdam, NY), 85

Lisa Maher (La Jolla, CA), 75

Robin C. Mangum (Sparta, NC), 65

Marsha McCarthy (Holliston, MA), 25

Sheryl Murray-Hansen (Portland, OR), 80

Lisa M. Naples (Doylestown, PA), 31, 93, 124

Matt Nolen (New York, NY), 56

Lisa Orr (Austin, TX), 31, 124

Matthias Ostermann (Quebec, Canada), 59, 87

Susan Papa (Midlothian, VA), 28

Carrie Ann Parks (Riverdale, MI), 126

Stephen Patt (Aguanga, CA), 24

Margaret Rattle (Sebastopol, CA), 126

Nausika Richardson (Dixon, NM), 57

Paul Sacaridiz (Chicago, IL), 82

Virginia Scotchie (Columbia, SC), 83, 128

Terry Siebert (Bainbridge Island, WA), 7, 55, 59, 93

Victor Spinski (Newark, DE), 71, 85

David Stabley (Bloomsburg, PA), 130

Irma Starr (Kansas City, MO), 86

Bernadette Stillo (Philadelphia, PA), 62

Nao T. Tajiri (Portland, OR), 123

Joan Takayama-Ogawa (Pasadena, CA), 62, 73, 74

Cheryl Tall (Stuart, FL), 133

Kathy Triplett (Weaverville, NC), 29, 81, 131

Kurt Weiser (Tempe, AZ), 63

John Werbelow (Gillette, WY), 84

Sarah E. Williams (Jamaica Plain, MA), 70

Lisa Woollam (Ontario, Canada), 29, 58

Mitch Yung (Branson, MO), 7, 21, 59

RECOMMENDED READING

Cameron, Julia. *The Vein of Gold: A Journey to Your Creative Heart.* New York: G.P. Putnam's Sons, 1996.

Carnegie, Daphne. *Tin-Glazed Earthenware: From Maiolica, Faience, and Delftware to the Contemporary.* Radnor, PA: Chilton Book Co., 1993.

Chappell, James. *The Potter's Complete Book of Clay and Glazes.* 1977. Reprint, New York: Watson-Guptill Publications, 1991.

Charleston, R. J. (Robert Jesse). *World Ceramics: An Illustrated History.* Edited by John Ayers [and others]. New York: McGraw-Hill, 1968.

Conrad, John W. *Advanced Ceramic Manual: Technical Data for the Studio Potter.* San Diego, CA: Falcon Co., 1987.

Csikszentmihalyi, Mihaly. *Creativity: Flow and the Psychology of Discovery and Invention.* New York: Harper Collins Publishers, 1996.

Cushing, Val. *Cushing's Handbook.* Alfred, New York: Alfred University, New York State College of Ceramics, 1997.

Faine, Brad. *The Complete Guide to Screen Printing.* Reprint, Cincinnati, OH: Writer's Digest Books, 1993.

Georgini, Frank. *Handmade Tiles.* Ashevillle, NC: Lark Books, 1996.

Lamott, Anne. *Bird by Bird: Some Instructions on Writing and Life.* New York: Pantheon Books, 1994.

Larson, Ronald. *A Potter's Companion: Imagination, Originality, and Craft.* Rochester, VT: Park Street Press, 1993; distributed in U.S. by American International Distribution Corporation.

Leach, Bernard. *A Potter's Book.* 3rd ed. London: Faber, 1976.

Rawson, Phillip. *Ceramics.* Philadelphia: Univ. of Pennsylvania Press, 1984.

Rhodes, Daniel. *Clay and Glazes for the Potter.* Rev. ed. Radnor, PA: Chilton Book Co., 1973.

Rossol, Monona. *The Artist's Complete Health and Safety Guide: Everything You Need to Know About Art Materials to Make Your Workplace Safe and Comply with United States and Canadian Right-to-Know Laws.* 2nd ed. New York: Allworth Press, 1996.

Scott, Paul. *Ceramics and Print.* Philadelphia: Univ. of Pennsylvania Press, 1995.

Speight, Charlotte and John Toki. *Hands in Clay.: An Introduction to Ceramics,* 3rd ed. Mountain Vie, CA: Mayfield Publishing Company, 1995.

Triplett, Kathy. *Handbuilt Ceramics.* Asheville, NC: Lark Books, 1997.

ACKNOWLEDGMENTS

The making of this book took the help of many people and was a process that amazed me in its synchronicity.

Thanks

To Chris Rich, who called me on a day that was full of possibility.

To Katherine Duncan, my editor, whose sense of humor, enthusiasm, understanding, and patience made the writing process enjoyable.

To Kathy Holmes, art director, whose composition of images and text created a beautiful book.

To Evan Bracken, whose thoughtfully created photos make the techniques easy to understand.

To Lark Books, whose commitment to art education enriches so many people's lives.

To the artists and galleries who supplied the work that composes the gallery of the book.

To Great Lakes Clay, Amaco Ceramics, and Minnesota Clay who contributed products for my demonstrations in Chapter Three.

To the faculty and students at Moraine Valley Community College for their inspiration and support.

To my teachers, students, and colleagues who have shared the path this last twenty years.

Special thanks to those friends and family whose love and nurturing have guided me:

To George Demarest.

To Kim Peters-Millman and Jill Peters for their constant reminders of the artist's way.

To Donna Wilshire, my model for never giving up.

In memory of Rebekah Wilshire, who gave me the gift of gratitude for every day.

To Stephanie Silk, whose friendship I treasure.

To Victoria, Daniel, Didier, and Diana.

To Val Cushing and all those at Alfred University that gave me a foundation in ceramics based on love and respect for clay.

To Deb Black and Michelle Dunn-Langosch.

To Halina Haywood, who has taught me to create from nothing.

INDEX